Contested Terrain

Contested Terrain

Diversity, Writing, and Knowledge

Edited by

Phyllis Kahaney
San Diego State University
San Diego, CA

Judith Liu
University of San Diego
San Diego, CA

Ann Arbor

THE UNIVERSITY OF MICHIGAN PRESS

Published in the United States of America by
The University of Michigan Press
Manufactured in the United States of America
♾ Printed on acid-free paper

2004 2003 2002 2001 4 3 2 1

A CIP catalog record for this book is available from the British Library.

ISBN 0-472-09786-5
ISBN 0-472-06786-9 pbk

Contents

Chapter 1

Introduction: Defining the Terrain

Phyllis Kahaney
San Diego State University
San Diego, CA

Judith Liu
University of San Diego
San Diego, CA

The idea for this volume emerged from a one-day conference held at the University of San Diego (USD) in which we searched for ways to integrate the efforts of the Writing across the Curriculum program with the movement to infuse the Cultural Diversity across the Curriculum program within the general college curriculum. At USD, Phyllis was responsible for the Writing across the Curriculum program, and Judith was responsible for the Cultural Diversity across the Curriculum program. By deciding to try an innovative approach to meld these two programs together, we sought to examine how using writing to explore issues of diversity could be incorporated into the college curriculum in a way that might allow for inclusion of voices that were more reflective of the changes occurring in American society. The result was a conference entitled "Writing across the Spectrum: Exploring Cultural Diversity through Writing." What emerged from the conference was a provocative discussion about how the Writing across the Curriculum movement per se was limited in its approach to broadening the intellectual horizons of college students. Ultimately, that discussion led to a political call for action that served as the impetus for this volume.

The chapters in this volume are situated in what we perceive to be a shift that has been taking place regarding the way language is used.

The authors are indebted to Monica Wagner for her care to detail in preparing the entire text. We thank Dr. Linn Bekins for her thoughtful reading and insightful comments. We extend special thanks to Donald P. Kelly for his invaluable assistance and critical analysis of this chapter.

This shift can be understood as the increased recognition among researchers in many fields of study that the use of language to represent reality is most often described as inherently political or social, or dialogic and constructed; as the way "valued knowledge" is learned through writing (i.e., using language as a bridge that connects the "who" of social practices to the "what" of cultural beliefs); and as moving beyond Michel Foucault's (1972) idea of "semiotic meaning" to an inclusion of Pierre Bourdieu's notion of "field," a view that stresses how individuals are positioned within structures of power and knowledge (Bourdieu 1985; Bourdieu and Wacquant 1992). In coming to more clearly understand how the activity of writing is rooted in these social, economic, and philosophical constructs, we began to envision a whole new way in which the activity of writing could be transformative.

Given this understanding, the challenge becomes one of moving away from a stand in which one group intentionally or otherwise marginalizes another in the name of an exclusive group identity, to a comprehension of how this exclusion takes place and how it may begin to be ameliorated. The authors in this volume argue that a frequent error made when discussing cultural diversity is that a negativity deriving from relativistic thinking arises. What is needed to correct this relativistic thinking is for teacher and student alike to take a moral stand that challenges deeply held beliefs. The ability to begin to see these beliefs and then take action to make changes is not an easy process. But through reflection and classroom practice, the authors have discovered that writing is a very useful way to do this, because it is an activity fostering development, interpretation, and inclusion.

The Power of Education

Informed by the Freirian definition of knowledge as a commodity, critical pedagogy has defined the act of writing as a political activity in which students are made to explore their social positions while coming to see that certain discourses privilege some groups while disparaging others (Freire 1972). Over the years, questions have been raised about whether or not this notion applies to the modern North American classroom (Graff 1991; Miller 1998). Further, much has been written arguing that the aims and processes of schooling are not neutral but influenced by relationships of power and authority that can be coercive and unequal (Giroux 1981; Bizzell 1992). In this way, when examining teaching and learning, what emerges is the view that the intention of education is to produce good citizens who will take orders and conform to what is expected of them.

However, if we try to understand education from the perspective of what it means to be a learner, different criteria emerge. Rather than issues of power and authority being most important, the making of meaning is understood in this context as being something not immediately present in one word alone. Meaning is thus made not so much from bracketing off content and focusing on form but rather as a process of division and articulation in which the discussion about meaning becomes as important as what is spoken about. Included in this definition is the understanding that meaning is made in the interaction between the text and the person reading—as a kind of dialogue or interactive process (Vygotsky 1978; Fish 1980; Tompkins 1980; Bakhtin 1981; Russell 1991; Gee 1999). Because meaning is made in interactivity, it is understood as something that is continually being constructed, torn down, and reconstructed, so that it is never fixed (Bakhtin 1981; White 1985). Seeing meaning as something that is in flux requires that the meaning maker see knowledge, then, as something that is created in a given community, at a given time, in a given way. This understanding is different from the perspective in which meaning is affixed to a social or political position.

It is not sufficient to see the language used in writing as political in the usual sense. Writing should also be seen as a social activity that interconnects the way we think about things to the social rules implicit in the activity of writing. One way to look at this view of writing is to look at Gee's (1999) definition of social goods, particularly the social good of "valued knowledge" and how it is learned through writing. Because the collection of data, the diffusion of information, and the creation of knowledge are the reasons academia exists—and because, with few exceptions, this knowledge necessarily becomes "written knowledge" (Bazerman 1988)—mastering a discipline requires an understanding of the meaning of the discursive and generic elements that combine to constitute that discipline. This act of understanding what is relevant in any given discipline requires that a writer (or a reader) be involved with and be knowledgeable about previous "conversations" within a given discipline (i.e., be aware of certain texts and the contexts surrounding those texts). The activity of writing, with this kind of awareness, aids the transformation into self-reflexive knowledge.

Besides learning the politics of the conversations embedded in the written word, as well as the getting and dissemination of valued knowledge in the activity of writing, it is also necessary to explore the meaning of *discourse.* For Foucault (1970, 1972, 1980), the definition of *discourse* entails transmission of semiotic meaning; anything written or spoken or communicated through signs involves discourse. There is one important proviso to this definition: Foucault is primarily interested in written knowledge that requires specialized training to understand its specialized language and vocabulary. This meaning of *discourse* can be said to be the circulation of ideas within a particular field of knowledge, giving those in power within that discipline the authority to define the parameters of the discipline. As Foucault notes (1970), the epistemic nature of discourses changes over time. This view relates to this volume in that our effort here is an attempt to change *epistēmē,* the way people think.

Another way of looking at the shift that has taken place in our understanding of the way language is used can be found in Bourdieu's (1985) theory of field. By understanding that the internal structure (or "field") in each discipline is governed by its own laws, its own hierarchy, and that all fields are competitive arenas concerned with the production or reproduction of the society/discipline for the distribution of its rewards, we begin to understand that inclusion means expanding the field of academia. Hence, acculturating to a field means acculturating to a "discourse community." Implicit in this acculturation process is the understanding that to perform well in today's job market, it is necessary for workers not only to have competent language skills but also to be able to know into which contexts to put information. From our perspective, competition arises when the discursive playing field is leveled and individuals have an equal chance of participating in the "game" (the dialogue), whereas conflict arises when individuals are excluded from participating in the game and must resort to political sniping to be heard from the periphery of the field. From this perspective, students would do better if the fact that there is a field or discourse community were made explicit so that they could understand from the outset that discourse not only involves the use of language but incorporates the politics of language, as well.

From this brief look at the work of Foucault and Bourdieu, it becomes apparent that discourses are historically situated—they do not exist out of time; discourse writ large (i.e., the scientific method) can be seen as monolithic, powerful, and epistemic (Foucault), but that does not mean that at the level of a disciplinary field of study, the predominant discourse cannot ever be challenged (Bourdieu). In fact, the kinds of writing suggested by the authors in this volume can go a long way toward challenging closely held beliefs that often appear sacrosanct.

What Does It Mean to Be a Successful Writer?

Exploring this shift is all the more critical because the recent mandates to hold schools accountable for producing students who can meet standards and who can pass certain tests is in direct conflict with the skills students will actually need when they are out in the workforce. Instead of hiring good citizens who can perform rote tasks, as employers often did a generation ago, those who hire in the present job market are more likely to look for workers who can deal with complex issues, be creative problem solvers, and think critically. In an increasingly complex world, those who succeed will be people who can move from the known to the not yet known and create new ways of doing a job or refining existing technology. This means that workers not only must have competent language skills but also must be able to know into which contexts to put information. The study and use of language thus becomes a system in which a country's economic health is dependent not only on the social and the political but also on the educational.

The problems of defining the nature of writing and the teachability of writing have been explored at length by scholars in the fields of composition and rhetoric, especially in the Writing across the Curriculum movement. The Elaine Maimon/C.H. Knoblauch and Lil Brannon debate of the 1980s underscores the continuing concern professionals working in this movement have had about whether or not writing across the curriculum facilitates entry into the discourse community that characterizes a given discipline by inculcating the necessary generic meanings that are at the heart of that particular discipline (Knoblauch and Brannon 1984; Maimon 1980).

A prevalent view in the Writing across the Curriculum community at that time was that expository writing is a set of preexisting structures through which a novice writer is socialized into a new discourse community (Maimon 1979). One form such structures take would be decentralizing composition courses from the domains of English departments; writing would be taught by various professionals in various disciplines. This model held that by learning the rules of writing in a given discipline, a student in that discipline could be taught to produce a discipline-specific text. When students learn the generic conventions of writing in a given discipline, Maimon argued (1979, 369), their "cognitive overload" is reduced, thus allowing them to "acquire better control over the written code used by educated people."

But according to Knoblauch and Brannon (1983, 465), this view that offers "ideal models for the presentation of knowledge in different fields" is not as helpful to novice writers as it might appear at first glance. Knoblauch and Brannon argued that rather than enabling students to understand the meaning and acquire the knowledge of their disciplines, teachers tend to add writing assignments at the periphery of their courses, so that writing becomes "perfunctory verbal exercises" (466). Because many faculty members in such fields as biology or art history are nervous about teaching writing, their tendency is to look to their colleagues in English departments for help. Thus, English departments retain control over how writing is taught and valued elsewhere. Because students often perceive as peripheral the kinds of writing assignments that emerge from English departments, they tend to find the activity of writing barren and ritualistic, seeing writing as recapitulating what everyone already knows or existing as mere exercises in the correct use of grammar and punctuation. According to Knoblauch and Brannon, the value of writing in any course "should lie in its power to enable the discovery of knowledge" (466); that is, writing should not be used as a means for students to recapitulate information in an unreflected manner, because only through reflection can information be transformed into useful knowledge.

While it turns out that both sides in the argument have been at least partially correct in their assessments of the practicality of implementing Writing across the Curriculum programs (Yancey and Huot 1997), this fact does not preclude the degree of intellectual overlap between the ideal of writing across the curriculum and the problems inherent in its implementation. Both sides are concerned with making students more knowledgeable about a discipline so that they can become more familiar with the written generic components that define the boundaries of the discourse community they are seeking to enter.

Using writing as a tool to discover what is worth knowing, rather than just as a way of reproducing knowledge, makes the act of knowing an activity, not simply a condition or a state. Learning in activity is very different from knowledge as an artifact, an inert body of information (Russell 1991). When students are given writing assignments that require them to interact with information in their given field, they learn to think like a person in that field of study and so move past formal constraints to the discovery of knowledge. In this way, students learn to translate thinking processes into professional conventions that they eventually need to master when learning to write in a new field of inquiry.

One purpose of this volume is to begin to flesh out the key concepts that mark the field of study when trying to use writing as a way of infusing cultural diversity into the curriculum. Another focus of this volume is to make explicit the fact that when a writer sets out to convince a reader to adopt a particular point of view, certain kinds of logical strategies (e.g., persuading the reader to accept a given perspective) as well as social conventions (e.g., providing cultural and historical contexts, as well as correct usage) are implicit in the text. Though professors often declare that the reason a student paper is unsuccessful is that the citations are wrong or the grammar is poor (Mathison and Freeman 1998), the authors in this volume attempt to show that these responses to student writing often mask the deeper problems of personal and social constructs versus socially independent absolutes. The chapters in this book are situated within the social constructivist perspective, which holds that there are no absolutes and that reality and hence meaning are human creations. Thus, the construction of meaning is a multilevel and multidimensional endeavor between readers and writers.

This fact is not readily apparent to student writers, who tend to regard any criticism as nit-picking. Where instructors generally understand the construction of meaning as the critical issue, students often fail to comprehend the connection between what they say and how they say it. Students tend to see assignments as a series of tasks that lead to a grade, rather than as a process that is designed to lead to a greater expertise in the use and power of language. This constricted view of the activity of writing does not permit some student writers to see that an important goal of the writing they do is to engage in a dialogue with the reader, to understand that the written knowledge they produce is a collaborative undertaking that is a seemingly endless dialectic (Bazerman 1988).

To understand the construction of meaning, it is crucial to look at texts, writers, readers, and contexts. By doing this, the way that readers interpret what they read becomes discernible. This view holds that the nature of texts (for both readers and writers) is that they are not fixed. Because meaning is constructed, it is made within the context of a society, a culture, or an individual and is always in the process of being "constructed, torn down, and reconstituted" (White 1985). In this view, language cannot be separated from meaning, and we find ourselves rooted in the reader-response argument, where we see language from the Wittgensteinian perspective of "a kind of social action rather than a system of referential tags" (Wittgenstein 1974, 291).

From this perspective, interpreting writing tends to be less about language as a fixed entity and more about language as a "fluid" entity that is continuously constituted and reconstituted by people and their culture. If this is the case, the implication is that there would be no simple solution to language's complexities. One such complexity is that of negotiating truth—how we know what to believe or not to believe as factual when reading and writing. Classical rhetoric, for example, was based on the belief that thought equaled logic. Modern rhetoric does not make the supposition that thought is always logical. A central task of modern rhetoric is constructivist; texts are deconstructed and then built up, ad infinitum. Where the Greek dialectic assumed norms that led to universal truths, the dialectic of modern rhetoric is not based on a belief in norms. Because this construct is usually seen as socially driven, truth, then, is perceived as relative—something that is interpreted.

The tendency of modern rhetoricians to view language as both a social and a cultural phenomenon underscores the ways in which the use of language can be interpreted. One way of understanding the growth of the writer from novice to expert is to explore the way these beginners are acculturated into their community. Like tourists in a foreign country, students learning to write do a lot of looking around, make many false starts, mimic what they see their "hosts" doing, and, with increasing degrees of success, are finally able to create their own documents. According to Patricia Bizzell in her (1982) study of cognition and writing, composition theory should be seen not as wholly inner-directed or outer-directed but as a combination of both the cognitive/developmental and the social, an "interpretive community" (to use Stanley Fish's term) "whose language-using habits," Bizzell argued, "are part of a larger pattern of regular interaction with the material world." Bizzell continued, "Because this interaction is always an historical process, changing over time, the community's conventions also change over time" (226). A discourse community, then, is interactive (between self and others), rule-governed (the rules emanate from the person and from the society and are changeable and in flux), and open to interpretation (meaning is open to discussion).

In attempting to describe what it means to have a well-written text, then, several points must be taken into consideration. It would be important to examine the nature of the discourse community by which a text is produced and read. It would be equally important to describe the ways that the readers of texts interact with the text. Finally, it would be helpful to note the function of rhetoric within those discourse communities. In this regard, assignment making is important. The best assignments will engage students to think critically about what they understand to be true, so that they will be able to question conventional wisdom, reflect on stated arguments, and internalize new ideas.

What Is the Contested Terrain?

The debate in English departments over the meaning and purpose of writing has its counterparts in other disciplines' questions about the purpose of education. Implicitly or explicitly, it can be argued that education has a trifurcated role. First, because education is designed to acculturate individuals into a given society, students are taught to accept a particular belief system—an ethos—that defines how "things" ought to be. Second, because education is designed to socialize individuals, students are taught to accept social practices—or worldviews—that define how "things" actually are. This move toward the acceptance of social practices is facilitated by what we normally view as education's third chief purpose: the intergenerational transfer of a corpus of knowledge. If a society is to continue, these acts of acculturation and socialization will continue also.

Underlying this view of the purpose of education are certain assumptions about education's role in society that are increasingly being called into question. For example, a set corpus of knowledge assumes the existence of certain facts and certain truths that are timeless and immutable (Bloom 1987; Hirsch 1987; D'Souza 1991; Cheney 1995). Acceptance of this view neglects a belief in the constructed nature of knowledge and meaning and has come under attack from groups whose cultural beliefs and social practices are not included in the existing curriculum. With the development of postmodern thought, these groups have sought to gain a voice in society's grand narrative.

This battle over inclusion marks the "contested terrain" in the title of this work.

It soon becomes apparent that despite the unity implied in the terms *American culture* and *American society*, a multiplicity of social and cultural differences have become manifested in the differentials in power, privilege, and knowledge that help to stratify society. These social contexts and stratifying variables involve, among other factors, a person's ethnicity, gender, sexual orientation, education, socioeconomic status, personal experiences, religion, and abilities and/or disabilities. Diversity refers to the recognition of the heterogeneity of cultures that compose a society. The range of cultures is manifested in all aspects of the daily lives of a community's or group's functioning and interactions.

Individuals in different social groups do not necessarily think of themselves in the same ways. For example, those who designate themselves as belonging to the dominant, white society most often talk about themselves in individualist terms, while those from other, often disenfranchised groups more often refer to themselves in collectivist terms (Blauner 1990). This means that identity is defined for the latter; their task is to learn to fit in with the existing parameters of identity. In other groups, identity is something for which an individual searches, with varying degrees of success.

The degree to which individuals are included in or excluded from a given community can be said to be a hallmark of the way and the degree to which individuals embrace or reject the hegemonic language usage. What is understood to be said and by whom it is said represent the power of authority that some groups will accept and others will reject. For example, in the ongoing debate about the Western canon, who gets included and who gets excluded has far-reaching implications for the whole of American society. What is considered by those with authority (professors, politicians, religious leaders) to be worth reading (and writing about) is more than which books are to be read. The canon symbolizes a battleground where what is at stake is represented by the questions: What does inclusion or exclusion from the canon mean? Who is to determine which texts are worth including and which are to be rejected? Ultimately, the battle involves the question, What is truth?

These questions encapsulate the unstated yet underlying fear concerning what will happen to American society when knowledge is not canonically given but is something that must be negotiated. Will this mean that all knowledge becomes relative? Are all ideas equal? Will this position lead to the cacophony surrounding cultural chaos and social anarchy? Challenging the canon is perceived by some as nothing more than a political activity that attacks what we really need to know (e.g., Hirsch 1987). Thus, challenging the canon becomes revolutionary because it means including in the college curriculum a corpus of knowledge that has traditionally been excluded from it. In essence, the debate centers on what it means to be an American in general.

This volume, then, roots itself in the position that reading and writing are political activities. We firmly believe that adding Cultural Diversity across the Curriculum programs to the college curriculum in a substantive manner will help mitigate the problems inherent in any disciplinary discourse community—that is, its exclusivity, its restrictiveness, and its particularistic knowledge. Genuine inclusion is the only means to overcome these problems. As yet, though, the simple inclusion of ideas is not enough. We call for a new way of creating discourse communities, one that changes the rules and regulations about the way meaning is made in the various academic disciplines by opening discourse to include more voices—voices that are more reflective of the changes occurring in American society. We believe that writing is the crucial element in accomplishing this transformation, since it is through writing that individuals begin the process of reflection that converts information into useful knowledge; it is through writing that students can best grapple with ideas and make sense of them.

These things—historicity, the notion of truth, how knowledge is to be understood, and dialogue—are addressed in this interdisciplinary volume in many ways. In part 1, four authors examine theoretical issues informing cultural diversity and writing. In chapter 2, John Wills and Hugh Mehan suggest that in the present debate about cultural diversity, a new perspective is needed. For example, instead of simply inserting into the curriculum minority representatives who contributed to important historical moments, it is useful to take a sociological perspective so that the institutions and societal issues of the times are understood. In this way, minorities become part of the totality that is American history, rather than merely being add-ons to a particular historical view. To do this successfully, it is important for the reader and writer of history to understand that historical facts are not either-or situations (e.g., were the Aztecs "good" or the Spanish "bad"?). Rather, what is called for is creating a learning environment that demonstrates that more than one group played important roles in history and that many voices contributed to the evolution of American society. Without such a perspective, Wills and Mehan argue, nothing more than a casual foray into a multicultural perspective can take place. This limited understanding is bound to lead to one of three pitfalls and traps: "cultural tourism," in which the cultural attributes of a specific group are studied; drifting "out of the mainstream," where the focus is on notable individuals and events that situate them outside of the historical events being examined; and "discontinuity," in which underrepresented groups are not part of the ongoing historical narrative. Because of these problematic ways of looking at history, the learner's attention is focused on culture and not on social interaction in history. Wills and Mehan conclude by exhorting the reader to take action, arguing that now that ignorance of the core issues can no longer be used as an excuse for not making important curricular revisions, changes should be made.

In chapter 3, Tom Fox focuses on the history of "institutionalized" practices of composition, exploring such issues as the way literacy was used to oppress slaves, the ways that freedmen's schools were ultimately developed in the antebellum South, and the subsequent ways in which literacy education from that period until now has failed to generate social or political power for today's African Americans. The reader is left with the impression that as things now stand, those who are involved with writing and composition practices can often do little more than reproduce the existing oppressive social structures of past times, causing literacy to become an assertion of a particular identity. For this reason, studying the history of literacy outside of institutions can help us understand how writing in present times can and should include the voices of marginalized groups.

With a powerful, personal voice, Gail Pérez chronicles in chapter 4 her journey in transforming her own pedagogy to include the voices of marginalized groups and the question of what constitutes "knowledge." She argues that including the voices of the "other" in postformal education not only challenges what Wills and Mehan define as the "core curriculum" but also provides a meaningful way by which marginalized groups can be included in the production of knowledge. In making this argument, she performs three important services for the reader. First, she establishes a historical link between critical pedagogy and ethnic studies. Second, she discusses the need for reinventing the way we teach ethnic texts. Finally, she proposes developmental models for creating and using writing assignments. In all these ways, she urges the use of praxis.

In part 2 of the volume, the focus moves from chapters that give a theoretical overview to chapters that offer concrete, practical examples of how to use writing as a tool for introducing elements of cultural diversity into the university curriculum. The first of these chapters, chapter 5, by Franklin Ng, is based on Ng's experience as an anthropologist and asks the question, What information is worth knowing? Ng points out that the debate about the canon, while heated and sometimes emotional, can also prove to be enlightening and beneficial to the process of learning. Specifically, Ng discusses creating for largely second-generation Asian American students class assignments that challenge the idea of political correctness, especially the implicit acceptance in many Asian communities of racial hierarchies and class bias. By making explicit the implicit and often hidden belief systems of his students' families and community leaders, Ng encourages his students to explore similarities and differences between and among the various communities in which they live, thus encouraging critical thinking about American culture and, by association, about what it means to be an insider or an outsider in any group. Finally, Ng argues that teachers have to be more directed in the assignments they give to their students. Such a directedness helps students to bridge the gap between personal narrative and academic argument and between writing and cultural diversity.

In chapter 6, in further exploring how using writing intersects with fostering a multicultural perspective, Terri Hasseler and John Bean first define what is meant by the term *diversity* and then argue that giving multicultural writing assignments can help articulate—and complicate—students' thinking about multicultural issues, by introducing them to diverse ways of thinking and encouraging deep examination of their lives with respect to diversity and difference. Hasseler and Bean suggest that the problem with the traditional, argumentative essays that students are usually assigned is that such assignments often cause students to "shut out arguments that contradict their own views" and to fail to "seriously imagine other points of view." This is a problem, the authors explain, because it avoids truth seeking; students strive for victory instead of trying to determine truth. Another problem that arises when teachers assign the traditional essay is that students tend to use information from research texts as definitive and unassailable, rather than as authored and negotiable; such an insider/outsider conflict, which arises from more of an insider/outsider model, tends to make students uncomfortable with controversy. To overcome this problem, Hasseler and Bean have created an extensive appendix to their chapter, providing examples of assignments constructed in a way that will lead students to higher levels of understanding.

Mark Waldo and Amanda Espinosa-Aguilar also focus on assignment making, arguing in chapter 7 that well-written assignments can make all the difference between a well-crafted or a poorly constructed paper. They stress that the most important factor for successful paper writing, especially about topics that are related to cultural diversity, is clarity of assignment, and this is true for all classes in all subject areas. Making clear, concise assignments forces students to struggle with meaning as they work to understand the information they are interacting with, and it enhances critical-thinking skills, memory, and cognitive development.

In chapter 8, how students best learn is of primary concern in Steven Hartwell's discussion about how to address the issues of gay and lesbian students in the classroom. Hartwell first explores the relationship between cognition and affect, then moves on to metarules and metathinking, explaining that one problem in addressing gay and lesbian issues consists of the unspoken but pervasive "rules against knowing about certain rules" (Laing 1971, 111). This problem manifests itself in a form of cognitive dissonance where many students who hold onto a belief that all people should be granted equal rights do not let go of the conflicting belief that gays should not have equal rights. This inconsistency between stated belief and action taken is difficult to address, Hartwell asserts, by the usual classroom means—discussion, asking probing questions, and so on. Instead, Hartwell asserts that when addressing these issues in his law classes, the most productive way of penetrating students' resistance in this area is to assign an array of writing assignments and exercises. As Hartwell states, "when conflicting thoughts are expressed in writing, the dissonance is greater." This dissonance is a positive factor, because writing about what is taboo for them causes students to interact with their beliefs in new and different ways. In the wake of this exploratory writing, students can begin to change their minds, because they learn a form of counterattitudinal advocacy. The teacher is an important factor in this process; thus, teachers need to be aware of their own beliefs and then to teach in a way that is both persuasive and ethical. Such teaching does four things for students: (1) it openly reveals personal biases and political agendas; (2) it informs students about how the particular subject at hand fits into a larger political debate; (3) by acknowledging error and doubt and encouraging dissent, it fosters an avoidance of deception and distortion; and (4) it is absent of a predetermined ethical outcome.

In chapter 9, Min-Zhan Lu provides an overview of the volume by focusing on two conversations she sees emerging from the essays. The first conversation, arising from part 1, concerns the importance of incorporating texts that have been traditionally excluded by the academy. The second conversation, arising from part 2, concerns how professors can assist students in being more reflective about their own understanding of diversity issues through the use of writing assignments. By analyzing how the authors in this text add their voices to the conversation and how readers of the text might use the volume, Lu shows various ways in which writing about diversity issues can help teachers and students alike become more knowledgeable writers.

WORKS CITED

Bakhtin, Mikhail. 1981. *The dialogic imagination.* Ed. Michael Holquist. Trans. Caryl Emerson and Michael Holquist. Austin: University of Texas Press.

Bazerman, Charles. 1988. *Shaping written knowledge: The genre and activity of the experimental article in science.* Madison: University of Wisconsin Press.

Bizzell, Patricia. 1982. Cognition, convention, and certainty: What we need to know about writing. *Pre/Text* 3, no. 3: 65–92.

———. 1992. *Academic discourse and critical consciousness.* Pittsburgh: University of Pittsburgh Press.

Blauner, Bob. 1990. *Black lives, white lives: Three decades of race relations in America.* Berkeley: University of California Press.

Bloom, Allan. 1987. *The closing of the American mind: How higher education has failed democracy and impoverished the souls of today's students.* New York: Simon and Schuster.

Bourdieu, Pierre. 1985. The social space and the genesis of groups. *Social Science Information* 24, no. 2:195–220.

Bourdieu, Pierre, and Loïc J. D. Wacquant. 1992. *An invitation to reflexive sociology.* Chicago: University of Chicago Press.

Cheney, Lynne V. 1995. *Telling the truth: Why our culture and our country have stopped making sense—and what we can do about it.* New York: Simon and Schuster.

D'Souza, Dinesh. 1991. *Illiberal education: The politics of race and sex on campus.* New York: Free Press.

Fish, Stanley. 1980. *Is there a text in this class?* Cambridge: Harvard University Press.

Foucault, Michel. 1970. *The order of things: An archaeology of the human sciences.* New York: Pantheon.

———. 1972. *The archaeology of knowledge and the discourse of language.* Trans. A. M. Sheridan Smith. New York: Pantheon.

———. 1980. *Power/knowledge: Selected interviews and other writings, 1972–1977.* Ed. Colin Gordon. Trans. Colin Gordon et al. New York: Pantheon.

Freire, Paulo. 1972. *Pedagogy of the oppressed.* Harmondsworth, UK: Penguin.

Gee, James Paul. 1999. *An introduction to discourse analysis: Theory and method.* London and New York: Routledge.

Giroux, Henry A. 1981. *Ideology, culture, and the process of schooling.* Philadelphia: Temple University Press.

Graff, Harvey J. 1991. *The literacy myth: Cultural integration and social structure in the Nineteenth Century.* New Brunswick, NJ: Transaction.

Hirsch, E. D., Jr. 1987. *Cultural literacy: What every American needs to know.* Boston: Houghton Mifflin.

Knoblauch, C. H., and Lil Brannon. 1983. Writing as learning through the curriculum. *College English* 45:465–74.

———. 1984. *Rhetorical traditions and the teaching of writing.* Upper Montclair, NJ: Boynton/Cook.

Maimon, Elaine. 1979. Talking to strangers. *College Composition and Communication* 30, no. 4:364–69.

———. 1980. Cinderella to Hercules: Demythologizing writing across the curriculum. *Journal of Basic Writing* 2, no. 4:3–11.

Mathison, Sandra, and Melissa Freeman. 1998. *The logic of disciplinary studies.* Educational Resources Information Center, report series 2:33. Albany: National Research Center on English Learning and Achievement, State University of New York at Albany; Washington, DC: United States Department of Education, Office of Educational Research and Improvement.

Miller, Richard E. 1998. The arts of complicity. *College English* 61, no. 1:10–28.

Russell, David R. 1991. *Writing in the academic disciplines, 1870–1990: A curricular history.* Carbondale: Southern Illinois University Press.

Tompkins, Jane, ed. 1980. *Reader-response criticism: From formalism to post-structuralism.* Baltimore: Johns Hopkins University Press.

Vygotsky, Lev. 1978. *Mind in society.* Ed. Michael Cole, Vera John-Steiner, Sylvia Scribner, and Ellen Souberman. Cambridge: Harvard University Press.

White, James Boyd. 1985. *Heracles' bow.* Madison: University of Wisconsin Press.

Wittgenstein, Ludwig. 1974. *Philosophical grammar.* Ed. R. Rhees. Trans. A. Kenny. Berkeley: University of California Press.

Yancey, Kathleen Blake, and Brian Huot. 1997. *Assessing writing across the curriculum: Diverse approaches and practices.* Greenwich, CT: Ablex.

Part 1

Chapter 2

Recognizing Diversity within a Common Historical Narrative: Culture, History, and the Study of Social Life

John S. Wills
University of California, Riverside
Riverside, CA

Hugh Mehan
University of California, San Diego
San Diego, CA

Debate about the history and social studies curriculum, part of the "culture wars" that gained public attention in the 1980s, has been concerned primarily with appropriate course content. Essentially, the debate has turned on these questions: Should courses in U.S. schools present a common narrative, one that presumably unites all citizens by celebrating the achievements of Western civilization? Should schools open up the historical narrative to include the contributions of people who have been omitted, most often women and minorities? Should schools participate in the struggle for cultural justice and seek to advance civil rights and democratic public life?

We contend that the current debate about the curriculum masks deeper issues, the most fundamental of which are represented by the questions: How is a society constituted? What differences make a difference in constituting a society? More specifically, who are we as Americans? Who do we include in the narrative of the history of American society? Is there a common, integrated narrative of American history that unites us as a people and a nation?

We wish to acknowledge the helpful comments of Michael Apple, Gary Hart, Phyllis Kahaney, Judith Liu, and Lisa Rosen.

A debate about epistemology also lurks beneath the surface of this discussion. On one hand, "common culturalists," who call for a common historical narrative, often treat history (i.e., knowledge) as natural, fixed, context-free, and timeless. On the other hand, multiculturalists, who call for an expanded view of history, introduce alternative and competing narratives, which in turn lead to a different conception of history—one that is perspectival, constructed, and relative to historical setting and context.

Our understanding is that school knowledge, including historical knowledge, is socially constructed. The teaching and learning process has often been informed by a model of cultural transmission, in which teachers transmit school knowledge, located in the curriculum, to passive students, who consume this knowledge with varying degrees of accuracy. In opposition to this unidirectional understanding of teaching and learning, we argue that school knowledge emerges in the interaction among administrators, teachers, students, and the variety of school texts that are used in instruction. While the determination of what counts as school and historical knowledge is a social and cultural accomplishment, this negotiation is not an even or level process. Teachers and other state-sanctioned officials have more authority than do students in defining what counts as legitimate or useful knowledge in classrooms.

In this chapter, we provide some orientation concerning the debate about the history and social studies curriculum. This discussion is not intended to be a definitive review of the debate or of the literature. Instead, our intention is to present the context in which the practices we analyze were conducted and to discuss the important issues, concerns, and theoretical differences that have characterized the debate between multiculturalists and common culturalists, as well as that among multiculturalists themselves.

We also note that precious few of the participants in the debate have been very helpful in guiding teachers about how to teach history and social studies. Despite this lack of guidance from the national debate concerning what to teach, teachers have been working hard to inject previously missing information into their social studies and history curriculum. Unfortunately, teachers attempting to diversify their curriculum have fallen into a number of traps.

After reviewing the consequences of those difficulties, we propose an alternative perspective on the teaching of history and social studies.

This perspective maintains the continuity of a unifying historical narrative (albeit one that emphasizes the struggle for civil rights instead of a celebration of a democracy achieved, a possession that must be protected and revered) while including previously omitted voices as active participants in significant historical events.

The Debate over Reform in the History and Social Studies Curriculum

The debate over the content of the history and social science curriculum, in both higher education and K–12 education, has raised fundamental questions about history, culture, and identity. Is history a fixed body of facts that exist "out there," or is it necessarily a continuing process of interpreting the past in the present? Is U.S. history a story of great individuals contributing to the glory of the nation, or is it a story of discrimination, oppression, and conflict between diverse groups? Are such characteristics as race, ethnicity, and gender fundamental and fixed, or are they fluid and socially constructed? Are racial and ethnic groups distinct cultural entities, or are cultural groups necessarily interdependent and coconstructed?

Asserting that the fundamental purpose of education is to unify society, a significant group of educators has argued that a historical, common core curriculum should be taught to all U.S. students. Hirsch (1987) and Bloom (1987) were among the first to call for a common core curriculum. They lamented the loss of a shared set of cultural facts, images, and allusions that enabled U.S. citizens to communicate effectively and understand each other. Hirsch traced the decline in shared knowledge to the adoption of value-neutral and value-relative curriculum in the 1960s, while Bloom blamed the elite universities for setting the current generation of students adrift on a sea of superficial and naive moral relativism. Education, they said, is no longer used to teach moral values. The way to overcome this value relativism, they said, is to teach a core set of ideas and facts to all elementary and secondary students in the United States.

The relevant texts in Hirsch's proposal to regain "cultural literacy" would be drawn from Western civilization, the core political values from American democracy, and the ethical values from a secularized version of the Judeo-Christian tradition, coupled with industriousness, honesty, and tolerance of others. The legal concepts would be drawn from the English legal tradition. The language for instructing students in cultural literacy would be English only. Hirsch's proposal reflects the position of many opposed to multicultural education who see the relativism of beauty, reason, truth, and merit as a central and threatening feature of this reform effort. Educators and parents who believe that there are a set of values derived from "Western civilization" that persevere, that transcend, argue against the anthropological idea, incorporated within multiculturalism, that measures of human achievement are bound by history, culture, and context.

While Hirsch and Bloom worried about the ability of education to prepare students to communicate effectively in U.S. society, others supported a common core curriculum as a means for addressing what they saw as a threat to U.S. dominance in the global economy. Citing numerous national and international academic surveys that showed U.S. students performing poorly when compared with their German and Japanese counterparts, they believed a common core curriculum would enable students to accumulate the necessary knowledge to compete effectively. This call was supported by many members of the Reagan and Bush administrations, including former secretary of education William Bennett (1992), former assistant secretary of education Diane Ravitch (1990), former assistant secretary of education Chester Finn (1991), and the former chairman of the National Endowment of the Humanities, Lynne Cheney (1995).

Members of the Republican Party transformed the common core curriculum position from an intellectual debate into a concrete course of action. President Bush included suggestions from the National Governor's Conference in *Goals 2000* (1991), which called for national curriculum standards and a regimen of testing to see how well states, schools, and K–12 students were mastering skills in basic courses of study. At the same time, the National Center for History in the Schools was developing national standards for the teaching of U.S. and world history (Crabtree and Nash 1994a, 1994b), standards that emphasized student inquiry, research, and interpretation (Crabtree and Nash 1996). As discussed in Nash, Crabtree, and Dunn 1997, the National History Standards were effectively undermined by attacks from the conservative Right. Particularly effective were the attacks of Lynne Cheney, beginning with an editorial in the *Wall Street Journal*. In this editorial, Cheney attacked, among other things, the "grim and gloomy" portrayal of U.S. history in the National History Standards, as well as what she viewed as a politically correct history that ignored traditionally recognized leaders and groups while giving too much attention to women, minorities, and labor history.

Cheney (1995, 25) was particularly vitriolic in her condemnation of the relativism she saw contained in the National History Standards, arguing that they engaged in the "systematic denigration of America's Western heritage." Aspects of Western civilization, starting from Hellenic Greece and continuing through industrialization, were presented in a negative light, while aspects of Chinese, African, and Aztec cultures were celebrated, she said. Cheney was particularly upset that the National History Standards would encourage students to consider the architecture, labor systems and agriculture of the Aztecs but not their practice of human sacrifice. Also, the gathering of wealth would be celebrated when practiced by an African king but denigrated when practiced by American railroad barons. In lieu of this "postmodern," "politically correct" dogma, Cheney wanted to install a "celebratory history" in the schools, one that reminds students of the "true glory" of Western civilization and U.S. history.

The criticism of multicultural reform in history and social studies as producing history that is politically correct is shared by others, who worry that the multicultural approach to education is culturally divisive. Because multiculturalism sees race, ethnicity, class (and other group categories) as determinative of social action, Ravitch (1990) and Schlesinger (1992) argue that multicultural education encourages separatist tendencies. They cite Afrocentric curriculum as a particularly threatening case in point. D'Souza (1991) fears that in their enthusiasm to include omitted groups and achieve social justice, universities are becoming bastions of political correctness. Cheney (1995) says multicultural education's move to diversify the canon trivializes "the great works of Western civilization," because some lesser texts are included under the guise of a quota system.

In the debates over the history and social studies curriculum, common culturalists often treat multiculturalists as a unified group, but multiculturalists are in fact a diverse group advocating a diversity of approaches and pursuing different goals. Multiculturalists share in common their criticism of the traditional history and social studies curriculum, which they argue excludes people of color, women, people with disabilities, and gays from historical narratives and the literary canon (Sleeter and Grant 1987; Banks 1989; Nieto 1992; Banks and Banks

1995). Multicultural educators favor a robust pluralism—which, in its most extreme form, may include cultural separatism—and in general a diversified, highly contextualized curriculum that includes not only the standards of Western culture but also the historical and cultural experiences unique to the backgrounds of students (Massaro 1993).

Multicultural educators want the historical narrative to include the voices, experiences, and actions of diverse groups whose histories have been trivialized, misstated, or omitted. Such a narrative, they claim, would give a richer, fuller, less romantic and sanitized view of history. As a result, students would learn both that life, liberty, and the pursuit of happiness are foundational principles of American society and that racism, sexism, and other forms of prejudice make it harder for some groups to compete equally for these goals. Unless the facts of gender, ethnic, and racial discrimination are acknowledged, argue multicultural educators, their harmful effects cannot be ameliorated, and the goals of liberty and justice will not be achieved.

In the process of calling for a more inclusive historical narrative, multicultural educators tend to reject universal and foundational claims to truth, value, and beauty. Instead, they adopt a form of anthropological relativism, which argues that morality is rooted in a particular culture's history, conventions, practices, and beliefs. Therefore, they reason, the moral standards of one society cannot be subjected to criticism from the point of view of another society's standards or by appeal to one transcultural standard.

While there are, then, a number of underlying goals and beliefs that unite multiculturalists in opposition to common culturalists, there are important distinctions, divisions, and contradictions among theories of multicultural education (Torres 1998). While a somewhat oversimplified exercise, dividing multiculturalists between liberal and critical multiculturalists illuminates important differences in how multiculturalism is conceptualized and theorized. Critical multiculturalists (McCarthy and Crichlow 1993; McCarthy and Willis 1995; Kincheloe and Steinberg 1997; McLaren 1997; McCarthy 1998; Weil 1998) have criticized liberal multiculturalism for its failure to move beyond psychological understandings of racism and discrimination to recognize its structural dynamics, for its failure to interrogate the economic and political power of whiteness, and for promoting an essentialist view of culture and identity.

McCarthy and Willis (1995) identify three types of multicultural discourses on racial inequality that reflect the perspectives and goals of liberal multiculturalism. Discourses of cultural understanding embody the cultural relativism attacked by common culturalists and attempt to improve intercultural communication by stressing racial and ethnic pride and by fostering respect among diverse cultures. Discourses of cultural competence value cultural pluralism and seek to "build bridges" between diverse groups (Sleeter and Grant 1988), thereby reducing racial and ethnic antagonism. Discourses of cultural emancipation promote knowledge of the achievements of diverse groups as a means of reducing minority students' alienation from school, thereby improving these students' academic achievements. McCarthy and Willis's criticism of these models of multiculturalism, which reflects the general critique of liberal multiculturalism by critical multiculturalists, is that they conceptualize racism and discrimination as a psychological reality, a product of the values and attitudes of individual whites. In contrast, critical multiculturalists understand racism and discrimination as a product of power and the "differential structure of opportunities that helps to define race relations in the United States" (McCarthy and Willis 1995, 72).

As McCarthy and Willis note (72), these approaches to multicultural education pursue what Banks (1988) calls the "prejudiceless goal." Through sensitivity training, increased knowledge of diverse cultures, and an appreciation of the contributions of diverse groups and individuals to U.S. history and society, the values, attitudes, and beliefs of white students about people of color will change, and their actions will no longer be racist. Improving race relations through attitudinal change has been criticized as promoting psychological understandings of racism that fail to engage what critical multiculturalists view as the more appropriate target of multicultural education: differential access to structures of opportunity and institutional practices that empower whites at the expense of people of color (Sleeter 1993).

Critical multiculturalists are united by their criticism of the failure of liberal multiculturalism to address the unequal distribution of power in U.S. society (Kincheloe and Steinberg 1997; McLaren 1997) or to challenge the discrimination, inequality, and exploitation that characterize U.S. society (Ladson-Billings and Tate 1995). The structural dynamics of racism and discrimination are described by Lipsitz (1998, vii) as he discusses the "cash value" of whiteness in U.S. society (and hence whites' "possessive investment in whiteness").

> [I]t accounts for advantages that come to individuals through profits made from housing secured in discriminatory markets, through the unequal educations allocated to children of different races, through insider networks that channel employment opportunities to the relatives and friends of those who have profited most from present and past racial discrimination, and especially through intergenerational transfers of inherited wealth that pass on the spoils of discrimination to succeeding generations.

Liberal multiculturalism's focus on changing the racist values and attitudes of whites reduces racism and discrimination to an individual, psychological phenomenon and provides students with few resources for conceptualizing and working against institutional racism and inequitable economic and political structures in the United States.

Recognizing the power of white identity and the value of whiteness in U.S. society is another feature that separates liberal and critical versions of multiculturalism. While liberal multiculturalism has tended to focus on the raced or cultured other (learning about and appreciating the contributions of diverse racial and ethnic groups to society), critical multiculturalists have shifted the focus to whiteness in an effort to "make whiteness strange" (Dyer 1997, 4) and challenge whiteness as a "transparent racial identity" (Omi and Winant 1993). Efforts in teacher education (Sleeter 1993; McIntyre 1997; Lesko and Bloom 1998; Titone 1998) have attempted to make white identity visible to white teachers by problematizing whiteness and making visible the social, economic, and political privileges that whiteness entails. This is part of a larger effort to develop antiracist and multicultural educational practices that, by making the power and privileges of whiteness in U.S. society and culture visible to white teachers and students, can enlist whites as allies in combating racism, exploitation, and injustice while avoiding white guilt and hostility (McCarthy and Crichlow 1993; Jackson and Solis 1995; Kincheloe et al. 1998).

Finally, critical multiculturalists have challenged the conceptualization of culture and identity in liberal approaches to multiculturalism. Liberal multiculturalists have viewed minority groups as "distinct cultural entities" (Erickson 1991, as cited in McCarthy 1998), a conception of culture as distinct, separate, and fixed, which promotes a perspective that individuals are determined by their culture. This conception of culture and identity has been challenged by critical multiculturalists, who recognize the "interpenetration and radical hybridity" of cultures (McCarthy 1998, 155) and see cultures in an ongoing conversation in which they are interwoven and interdependent (Gates 1995). Under this conception of culture, identities are fluid and dynamic, coconstructed in the interaction between diverse groups and individuals, and not reducible to static and fundamental categories, such as race, ethnicity, or gender.

As a group, critical multiculturalists have much in common with advocates of critical pedagogy. The belief that systematic and pervasive discrimination plays an important part in American culture informs the views of both groups and their criticism of the way in which history and social studies are taught (see especially Aronowitz and Giroux 1985; Darder 1991; McLaren 1991; Giroux 1992; Giroux and McLaren 1989, 1994; Apple and Beane 1995; Sleeter and McLaren 1995). Conflict—not merit, choice, or personal effort—often explains the gap between white and nonwhite, rich and poor. Convinced that equality, justice, and social responsibility are the baseline conditions for a just society, critical multiculturalists criticize the unequal distribution of economic and educational resources among groups and say schools should participate in the struggle for cultural justice and should seek to advance civil rights and democratic public life. They agree with critical multiculturalists that curricular innovations are necessary to achieve equity, but educational changes are hardly sufficient, critical theorists assert, because the underlying inequalities in the society at large must be addressed if a just society is to be realized.

Major features of the critique of liberal multiculturalism by critical multiculturalists are consistent with our analysis, in the following sections, of the practices and approaches to multicultural education. Multicultural practices in schools and classrooms exhibit many of the deficiencies that critical multiculturalists see in liberal approaches to multicultural education. The curriculum in use promotes psychological understandings of racism and discrimination, constructs cultures as distinct and separate entities, and constitutes identity as a fixed characteristic of individuals.

We agree with many of the arguments of critical multiculturalists, particularly the need to understand the structural and institutional realities of racism and inequality in U.S. history and society. But our analysis is different because it is concerned with the ways in which common approaches to multicultural education undermine the goals of both liberal and critical multiculturalism. In effect, whether one's goal is to change the racist and discriminatory values and attitudes of whites by promoting the understanding and appreciation of diverse groups in U.S. history and society or to attack the structures and institutional practices that result in the inequitable distribution of economic and political power according to race and ethnicity by educating whites to the reality of the power of whiteness and white privilege in U.S. history and society, the practices we have observed in schools and classrooms render either goal unattainable. Exactly how this occurs in the curriculum in use is discussed in the following sections.

Traps and Pitfalls When Recognizing Diversity in the Curriculum

The debate about the history and social studies curriculum continues, and the gap between theory and practice also continues to grow. Critical multiculturalists have argued that structures of inequality, institutional racism, and white privilege in U.S. society and culture are the proper foci of multicultural efforts in education. At the same time, many, if not most, multicultural efforts in K–12 education continue to focus on celebrations of the contributions of diverse individuals and groups and on cultural festivals and fairs that reduce culture to foods, music, and other aesthetic differences. Some educators have made sincere efforts to go beyond these superficial approaches to recognizing diversity, but theory and research in multicultural education, along with the scholarly debate over the history and social studies curriculum, has provided little concrete direction for these teachers in developing curriculum.

We have examined middle school classrooms in which teachers have attempted to present multicultural histories of the United States (Wills 1994, 1996; Mehan et al. 1995). We have also made more casual observations of efforts by elementary and secondary schoolteachers to construct more inclusive versions of U.S. and world history. As these educators have attempted to recognize diversity in the curriculum, they have fallen into a number of traps. After we describe some of these pitfalls, we propose an alternative approach that can help teachers avoid these traps and that can provide the foundation for developing a robust multicultural history and social studies curriculum that embodies the social and cultural diversity that has always characterized the United States.

The Culture Trap in Reforming the Curriculum

"Cultural tourism" is one trap that awaits teachers who attempt to construct a more inclusive history. It involves representing underrepresented groups as cultural representatives and not as social or historical actors. Cultural tourism occurs when students are invited to study the cultural attributes of specific groups as static and fixed, rather than establishing the presence of members of cultural groups as social actors in particular historical events in U.S. history. Like tourists, students are invited to travel to foreign lands, learn about exotic people and places, and then return home to a place in which these people have no relevance in their daily lives. Yet the cultures that students are studying are not foreign to U.S. history but a part of it. When approaches to including diverse groups in U.S. history situate these groups outside of history, a student's knowledge of these groups resembles that of a tourist—knowledge of an exotic people, an "other," who may have no bearing on the student's own life or on U.S. history. As a consequence, students may conclude incorrectly that certain people, being members of cultural groups, have fixed cultural attributes, perhaps with a unique way of life and a unique and "different" perspective on the world.

For example, one eighth-grade teacher of U.S. history had her students conduct research on a variety of Native American tribes located in the Eastern Woodlands culture area during the colonial period of U.S. history. Based on this research, students produced "Fact or Fiction" books that addressed the material culture, religion, family life, clothing, social and political organization, and artistic expression of selected Native American tribes. The results of this engaging activity were a success as far as generating cultural information about Native American tribes, but this work failed to locate them in U.S. history or portray them as social actors in any specific historical events. For example, the students studying the Mohawk Indians reported that Mohawk children wore no clothing whenever possible, that the Mohawk did not live in tepees, that the Mohawk were skilled and fierce warriors, and that Mohawk Indians built bridges and skyscrapers in the United States and Canada because they had no fear of heights. But

Mohawk actions in particular historical events, such as the French and Indian War, were never mentioned. As a result, the Mohawks seem to exist outside of any narrative structure, sometimes in an elusive past, sometimes in an elusive present (e.g., as gangs of Mohawk Indians building skyscrapers and bridges), but never in the events and happenings that constitute U.S. history.

Brief essays that these students wrote on the origins of the United States reinforce our conclusion that they did not see Native American tribes as part of U.S. history. Seldom did the students mention Native Americans during the colonial period in their origin narratives, even though they spent a number of weeks studying and talking about Native American cultures during this historical period. The information they had learned about the cultures of Native American tribes was simply not relevant to the history of colonial America.

Because these portrayals of Native Americans exist outside of history, students have no knowledge of them as social actors in colonial America. What they thought of the white settlers, their interactions with these settlers, and the effects this had on their way of life are dormant topics. Even though these Native Americans can serve as cultural representatives of the Mohawk, Delaware, or other tribes studied, they cannot serve as examples of Native Americans as social or historical actors. If they were assigned the role of historical actors, students would have an opportunity to understand the history of Native American/white relations in the United States, which, in turn, is potentially useful knowledge for thinking about these relations in the present.

Other activities carried out in this classroom also fell victim to "cultural tourism," because they focused on cultural attributes rather than history or social action. The students read the novel *The Light in the Forest* (Richter 1953), about True Son, a white child abducted in a raid and raised by the Delaware Indians. As a young man, True Son is forcibly returned to his white family but refuses to renounce his Delaware heritage and attempts to return to his tribe. In a class discussion, students were asked to decide, having learned about Native American cultures, whether they would want to live with the whites or with the Native Americans if they found themselves in a similar situation as True Son. The class discussion was telling, because students explained that they would rather live with the Native Americans because they are "better people," with "better moral values," while whites are "kind of jerks" who like to "take over the land" and "control it." While this discussion was an opportunity for the students to explore their stereotypes concerning Native Americans, the discussion was, in fact, about deciding what kind of people Native Americans are and what kind of people whites are. The students concluded that Native Americans and whites are distinct kinds of people, because they have unique cultures that determine their outlook on the world and actions in it.

This incipient cultural determinism was also evident in a number of "Point of View" exercises that this eighth-grade teacher conducted with her students. The exercises, revolving around *The Light in the Forest*, emphasized how culture influences the different outlook of Native Americans and whites on the world, including whether to adapt to the land or to adapt the land to your needs; how Fort Pitt would seem like an "ugly, treeless prison" to Native Americans but a "safe home" to whites; and so on. These activities and exercises were useful in establishing the cultural differences between Native Americans and white settlers. But these activities were not useful in explaining the role these differences played in shaping the interactions between Native Americans and whites in colonial history.

This multicultural approach to recognizing diversity in history can lead teachers away from history; none of the exercises or activities dealing with Native Americans were focused on historical events, so they failed to place Native Americans into U.S. history. To the extent that Native Americans are present in this approach, they are present as cultural representatives. This multicultural approach exemplifies a Native American way of life and perspective on the world (of course, a problematic generalization) that is different from that of whites. But it tells students little to nothing about the role of Native Americans in U.S. history, their actions in specific events, and their interactions with other groups present in the colonial period. While these Native Americans are present in the curriculum, they are not actually present in U.S. history.

The Pitfalls of Including Diverse Groups in History

Critics of "traditional" U.S. history have pointed to the absence of women and people of color as evidence of the politics in what counts as good history. They have noted that women and people of color appear and disappear from the narrative during historical periods or in events of concern to whites. Chinese laborers work on the railroad, African

Americans are enslaved during the Civil War, and Native Americans are obstacles to be removed during the westward expansion, but these peoples remain virtually absent from the remainder of U.S. history (cf. Banks 1989; Sleeter and Grant 1991; Sleeter and McLaren 1995).

Many teachers attempt to recognize women and people of color by highlighting their contributions and accomplishments and allowing their previously missing voices to be heard. But these efforts can be flawed, because they unintentionally situate or position women and people of color outside the historical narrative being constructed or outside the specific historical events being examined. As a consequence, diverse groups (or, more accurately, their representatives) are rarely constituted as social actors in history but, instead, exist outside of history, as shining examples of their gender/race/ethnicity or as gendered or racialized commentators who are supposed to speak for their "people."

The troubles that can develop when teachers attempt to animate history with women and people of color are evident in a fourth-grade musical recounting the history of California. Beginning with Spanish exploration and concluding in the present, this musical has all the children in unison narrating the history of California and singing portions of popular songs related to the historical periods covered, interspersed with brief skits in which small groups of students act out specific historical events.

The Native American presence in California is noted early in the musical. Specific attention is paid to the culture of Native Americans, with the Chumash being identified by name. Represented events in the musical include the establishment of the mission system (noting that the padres, who were "well-intentioned," nevertheless "neglected and misunderstood the Indian ways of life"), the movement westward into California, the discovery of gold, statehood for California, the establishment of the transcontinental railroad, the San Francisco earthquake, the rise of the Hollywood film industry, and the agricultural wealth of California. This history of California is "traditional" in that women and people of color are virtually absent, except for the mention of thankfulness for "Chinese hard labor" in finishing the railroad.

The students conclude the musical by noting the contributions great individuals have made to California. They begin by naming great male authors: Mark Twain, Jack London, Robert Louis Stevenson, and others. Suddenly, students in the chorus loudly ask, "But what about the women?" They are rewarded with the names of three women authors: Helen Hunt Jackson, Mary Austin, and Ina Coolbirth. This challenge opens the door to including other women, specifically Isadora Duncan, the mother of modern dance; Lillian Gilbreth, an engineer and mother of twelve; Dorothea Lange, a photographer; and Amelia Earhardt. A few men of color are then mentioned as well: Jackie Robinson, a baseball player; Luther Burbank, a naturalist and experimenter; and César Chávez, whose claim to fame is not mentioned. This concludes the musical.

Significant about this inclusion of women and people of color is their location in this musical. The achievements and contributions of individual women and people of color are recognized outside and after the narrative of California history has been constructed. Only at the end of the musical, after the story of California finally arrives in the present, are these individuals brought on stage, introduced, and recognized for their accomplishments. The students in the musical and their parents and families in the audience witness history being made by others in the brief skits, while these notable individuals gathered on the stage in the conclusion are mere add-ons after the fact, after the story has been told. While these representative individuals are present on stage, they are not present in the narrative of U.S. history.

Another common multicultural approach used by teachers is to include women and people of color in history by allowing them to present their points of view in discussions of historical events. In role-playing activities, for example, small groups of students adopt the role of a notable figure in history and then comment on historical events from their unique perspective. Unlike the example of the musical on California history, this approach goes beyond the mere display of notable individuals by allowing individual women and people of color to discuss historical events, thereby providing them a somewhat more active role in the history curriculum. It is also useful in providing students with an understanding of history that is multiperspectival, allowing them to see how specific historical events were interpreted differently by different people.

This approach appeared in a discussion of the Boston Tea Party in an eighth-grade class in U.S. history. Small groups of students were assigned the role of important historical figures, including King George, Samuel Adams (a radical patriot), John Dickinson (a moderate colonist), Abigail Adams (a female colonist), Logan (an Iroquois

Indian), and Crispus Attucks (an African American). After reading some information on their individual and the group he or she represented, students were asked to comment on the Boston Tea Party from the perspective of these group representatives. Specifically, they were to address (1) how they felt about what happened in this event and (2) what they thought about the actions of the individuals in this significant historical event.

A number of issues made this activity difficult for the students. The information the students had to work with was primarily biographical, yet these voices were supposed to represent the perspective of their respective communities, about which the students had little or no information. Students lacked much of the historical information necessary to successfully reanimate these voices. Additionally, having one individual speak for an entire community silences the diversity within communities; if Crispus Attucks speaks for all African Americans, why did some African Americans support the colonists in the Revolutionary War, while other African Americans supported the British?

The absence of historical knowledge can plague any such role-playing activity. In terms of creating a more inclusive history, however, the most significant problem with this activity concerned the situation of these individuals as speakers. The events selected for discussion are "traditionally" important events. Such individuals as Logan and Attucks must speak about events that they themselves did not participate in. Logan and Attucks, unlike Samuel Adams, are not speaking as participants in the Boston Tea Party. Rather, both Logan and Crispus Attucks are asked to comment as representatives of the Native American and African American communities on the actions of radical patriots, such as Samuel Adams. In contrast, Adams gets to respond, "I think we did the right thing," speaking as an active participant in the Boston Tea Party.

Perhaps more importantly, the focus of this activity was not on history—on explaining what happened, who was involved, who did what, and the different perspectives that informed their actions. Rather, the focus was on getting the reactions of women and people of color to events that had already happened. This activity is not an exercise in explaining or understanding historical events but rather a lesson about multiple perspectives. As a result, such individuals as Logan and Attucks are positioned outside of history and constituted as commentators on the actions of others—individuals, such as Samuel Adams, who exist as actors inside important historical events. Finally, other activities in the classroom confirmed the role of patriots, loyalists, and moderates as historical actors, as the students read the Declaration of Independence, Paine's *Common Sense,* and other historical documents. These are the people who are quoted, pictured, and talked about in the students' textbook and other curriculum during this period in U.S. history. Again, while diverse individuals, such as Logan and Attucks, are present in the curriculum, they are not present as actors in the narrative of U.S. history.

The Discontinuity Trap

The *National Standards for Teaching History* (Crabtree and Nash 1996) and the *Framework for History and Social Studies* (California State Department of Education 1990) recommend that history be taught in such a way that students can use history to interpret current events. But when history is taught as discontinuous events, diverse groups appear and then disappear from the narrative in unexplained ways. Therefore, students have difficulty relating the relevance of the past to current events.

For example, one eighth-grade class spent a total of eight weeks studying the Civil War period, which included a detailed study of the experiences of African Americans as slaves in the South. The students learned a considerable amount about the brutalities, indignities, and injustices suffered by enslaved African Americans during this period in U.S. history, which presented them with clear lessons about the immorality of slavery. Yet when this teacher asked her students to connect the injustices experienced by African Americans under slavery to possible injustices experienced by African Americans in contemporary U.S. society (in reaction to the uprisings in Los Angeles in April 1992 following the acquittal of police officers for the beating of Rodney King), her students could not see the relevance of history in contemporary race relations.

These students had difficulty using the past to understand the present, because their knowledge of the injustices experienced by African Americans in U.S. history was anchored in slavery (Wills 1996). Other than their presence as slaves during the Civil War, African Americans were virtually absent from the U.S. history they studied. The only injustices these students thought African Americans experienced were associated with their enslavement. To these students, moreover, slavery was a problem that was "solved" many years ago. Therefore, these students did not see history to be relevant in thinking about the possible injustices suffered by African Americans in contemporary U.S. society. Slavery was a historically specific event; therefore, the injustice was also historically specific. Without a continuous history of African American experiences in the United States, connections between past and present injustices remained elusive.

Recognizing Diversity within a Common Historical Narrative

As we have suggested, efforts to include diverse groups in history have fallen into some unforeseen traps. Calls for recognizing diversity in the history and social studies curriculum have unintentionally led many teachers to focus their attention on cultural attributes and not on social action in history. We are arguing that the primary task of history and social studies education should not be the appreciation of cultural diversity, although an appreciation of cultural diversity may be a natural by-product of the approach we are advocating. Instead, we propose that the purpose of history should be to understand and explain the interactions of diverse individuals and groups in the past so that students can better understand the historical present of contemporary race and ethnic relations in U.S. society. This should include attention to culture, so far as culture is a resource or tool that mediates social action (Swidler 1986; Wertsch 1998). The history and social studies curriculum should help students understand the role of culture in action; this can be accomplished through the study of social life.

The Need for a Sociological Perspective

Focusing on cultural attributes often leads to the study of groups ahistorically, statically, and in isolation, rather than to the study of groups in interaction. History is made in interaction, as are the "distinct" cultures and identities of diverse groups, which are not fixed and separate but "interwoven and interdependent" (McCarthy 1998, 155). If history is to provide any lessons for the present, students need to examine and understand relationships to the past. In practice, this means that the history and social studies curriculum must enable teachers and students to construct narratives embodying the participation of diverse individuals and groups in U.S. history. Only through the creation of meaningfully inclusive narratives of history can the goals of multicultural reform, whether liberal or critical, be realized.

With this conception of history in mind, the task of a multicultural history and social studies curriculum becomes clear. Women and people of color must be visible in specific historical events to be visible in history. Furthermore, they must appear as active participants, that is, social actors who made sense of their circumstances and oriented their actions to others around them. Culture, while still present in the curriculum as a resource in structuring action, should no longer be the primary object of attention or be conceptualized as ascribed or permanent characteristics of individuals or groups.

The failure of the curriculum to establish a common narrative space in which diverse individuals and groups acted and interacted undermines the agendas of all in the multicultural debate in history and social studies. In what follows, we revisit the examples presented earlier to construct a sociological approach to history that includes women and people of color as participants in specific historical events. Our approach is sociological, because the absence of society in representations of the past was apparent to us in analyzing the curriculum in use in these schools and classrooms. Those teaching the history and social studies curriculum failed to construct a social space in which diverse groups acted and interacted in history. In response to this gap in the curriculum, we are proposing a history and social studies curriculum that advocates the study of history as social interaction.

Our sociological approach, focused on the study of social life in history and social studies, avoids the traps and pitfalls of previous efforts and is more likely to allow the construction of knowledge that is useful in achieving the goals of common culturalists and multiculturalists alike. On one hand, it recognizes diversity in the curriculum in ways that challenge reified and essentialist understandings of culture and identity. On the other hand, it advocates constructing a narrative of U.S. history organized around the struggle for civil rights, a unifying theme that unites diverse groups and individuals within a common historical narrative. An added benefit of this sociological approach is that it does not necessitate new curricular materials, only a shift in perspective, one that would enable teachers to make better use of the materials already at hand.

Recall the research on Native American cultures during the colonial period and the teacher's emphasis on cultural difference and point of view. Shifting the focus to an examination of social relations between Native Americans and white settlers would allow this teacher to get the same points about culture across and also to construct a more usable history of the colonial period. The novel the students read, *The Light in the Forest,* is rife with information on the relationships between the white settlers and the local Native American tribes. With more attention to this aspect of the novel, class discussions on point of view and cultural difference would look quite different. Students could use these differences in outlook and worldview to explain the actions of Native Americans and white settlers in this period of U.S. history. In this revised approach, the question is no longer whether culture makes a difference but what difference cultural difference made in the interactions between Native Americans and white settlers.

With a shift toward our sociological perspective, the students' "Fact or Fiction" books could be made a more useful activity. Rather than studying the cultural attributes of Native American tribes in isolation, attention could be redirected to examining facts concerning Native American and white relations during the colonial period, as well as the changes Native American and white contact wrought in the way of life and outlook of these Native American tribes. Here, there would be the possibility of moving beyond reified and static understandings of culture to recognize the heterogeneity of cultural groups and to then view culture as the product of ongoing interactions with other groups.

The focus on groups in interaction in specific historical events would also facilitate the meaningful integration of diverse groups into the history of California recounted in the fourth-grade musical. Recall that women and people of color were only showcased at the conclusion of the musical. At a minimum, shifting to a sociological perspective would make obvious the need to always situate individuals or groups in history and to portray what they were doing in concert with others. In this instance, the relations between Native Americans and the Spanish missionaries would be not simply mentioned but actually acted out. A similar change would occur with the Chinese labor used to build the railroads. Diverse groups would appear uniformly throughout the U.S. historical narrative—for example, Native Americans, Chinese laborers, and Mexican Americans in California during the gold rush. Shifting attention away from cultural attributes and toward social life would help students understand how history is made as diverse peoples come together in specific times and places.

Finally, this shift to a sociological perspective would affect the approach to integrating or recognizing multiple perspectives in the discussion of historical events. Teachers recognizing that history consists of social actors would be encouraged to choose for discussion certain kinds of event over others. Teachers would want to be careful to include events in which women and people of color could authentically speak as active participants. For example, rather than commenting on the Boston Tea Party, Crispus Attucks could debate Samuel Adams and Thomas Peters, an African American contemporary who allied himself with the British (Nash 1986), about whether or not African Americans should support the colonists or the British in the Revolutionary War. Juxtaposing Attucks, Peters, and Adams not only would constitute African Americans as actors in history but would also demonstrate to students the diversity of opinion within cultural, racial, and ethnic groups. This approach does not mean that a representative of every cultural, racial, or ethnic group would necessarily have to speak as a participant in every event. But when representatives of groups do appear, they would appear in appropriate historical events, constituting them as participants in history—speakers inside, rather than outside, the narrative of U.S. history.

Our sociological approach to teaching history adds a new dimension to what Banks (1989) has called the "transformative approach" to multicultural education. In Banks's approach, the curriculum is changed to enable students to view concepts, issues, events, and themes from the perspective of diverse ethnic and cultural groups. Central to this approach is the infusion of various frames of reference that provide students with a more complex understanding of U.S. history.

In fact, the activities in multiple perspective implemented in the classrooms we studied could be seen as examples of Banks's transformative approach. In the "Point of View" exercises, in particular, students were not simply exposed to the view of European colonists; they were asked to view issues and events from the cultural standpoint of different communities in colonial America. As we have seen, however, an approach involving multiple perspectives is not as transformative as one might imagine, because women, Native Americans, and African Americans are not situated as actors in U.S. history. Students learned about the existence of diverse perspectives, but these were divorced from any examination of the specific actions taken by these groups in historical events. While students learned about distinct cultural points of view, they did not learn how the actions of distinct groups, informed by their unique perspectives, contributed to the common history. The lesson is that while a transformative approach can be inclusive, it is not necessarily inclusive in any meaningful way unless the people who hold diverse perspectives are rendered as active participants in history.

Studying Social Life in History

The emphasis in our sociological approach to history is on social life. We believe that history should prepare and enable students to think critically about contemporary society by providing them relevant lessons from the past. To do this, history must help students understand and explain the interactions between diverse groups in specific historical events and during particular historical periods, because these events and periods constitute a common history.

Several features of our sociological approach will enable teachers to successfully recognize diversity in the history curriculum. First, the focus is on society, which means students should not study groups in isolation but, rather, groups in interaction. Society—whether equal or unequal, just or unjust—is constituted in this interactional space between groups. If students are going to learn lessons from history that are relevant to the present, this is where the lessons are going to be found. Therefore, diverse groups must always be situated in society. They must always be constituted as social actors who are interacting with others. The focus of inquiry in history and social studies must be on explaining and understanding these actions.

A second recommendation that emerges from our approach is situating diverse groups in time and space. Commentators who disagree on other points (e.g., Crabtree, Nash, and Cheney) agree that history is or should be, in the words of the *National Standards for Teaching History* and the California *Framework for History and Social Studies*, a "story well told." The history that we are advocating here, as a well-told story, is a sequence of events about the struggle for civil rights that adds up to the story of the United States. Teachers need to recognize that, along with their students, they are constructing a narrative of events about the struggle for social, economic, and political rights that constitutes U.S. history. This story about the struggle for rights tells us who we are as Americans (Gitlin 1995). If diverse groups are to be meaningfully included in the curriculum, they need to exist in this civil rights narrative. This means situating them as social actors, as active participants, in specific historical events and periods.

Third, our sociological approach to teaching history is necessarily conversational and, therefore, multiperspectival. The goal in learning about U.S. history is to understand and explain historical events. Why did this event turn out this way and not some other way? Explaining historical events necessitates including all the participants in them. Consider, for example, the Revolutionary War. Students will gain a deeper and richer understanding of this event if the views of women, African Americans, and Native Americans are included along with the views of those that are usually presented—white, male colonists and the British. After all, Native Americans were a force to be reckoned with in the colonial period. It mattered to the British and the colonists who they decided to support. Similarly, African Americans fought on both the British side and the colonists' side in the Revolutionary War. Therefore, understanding their participation will enrich students' understanding of this crucial and significant event in U.S. history. Studying history as social interaction, then, tells us not only about African Americans and Native Americans but about the views of the white colonists as well. A conversational or multiperspectival approach provides us the opportunity to learn about all the parties involved (Zinn 1980; Takaki 1993).

This sociological approach is evident in one sixth-grade teacher's attempt to integrate ancient civilizations. Faced with the problem of meaningfully including the civilizations of India and China in the more traditional study of Egypt, Greece, and Rome (i.e., Western civilization), this teacher developed a curriculum that focused on society and social life, rather than exploring the cultures of these groups. This teacher did not simply teach the food, clothing, music, and art of these groups, which is the approach so often taken by teachers attempting to include diversity in their curriculum (Cochran-Smith 1995; Sleeter and Grant 1987). Instead, she organized her students into small groups to research the daily life, religion, political organization, economic organization, or science and technology of one of these civilizations. Students had to work on several different civilizations throughout the year. Therefore, the group that reported on daily life in China would study the political organization in Egypt, science in China and India, and so on.

In this way, the students became familiar with different aspects of all five civilizations and were able to recognize the contributions and accomplishments of each. For example, each of the Egypt and China research groups declared that the country it researched was the first to make paper. This led to a comparison of dates to establish who was actually first, followed by a discussion of the nature of history and how history gets written. Similar discoveries occurred throughout the year, as students discovered equivalent scientific and technological accomplishments shared by these diverse civilizations. Because students continually studied all of these civilizations—rather than studying Egypt, Greece, and Rome (Western civilization) and then adding on the study of India and China if time permitted—India and China were recognized as equally significant civilizations in the ancient world.

During their investigations, students discovered the social interactions that existed between these civilizations. When entering this class, these students had perceived each civilization to be distinct, existing in isolation, with one civilization dying as another one rose to take its place. By the end of the school year, the students had gained the sense that these civilizations inhabited the same world over a period of many years and interacted with one another through trade, warfare, and cultural exchange. Instead of seeing these civilizations as distinct cultural groups, students came to realize, often on their own, the interconnectedness of these civilizations and cultures and of the mutual influences they had on one another. Locating these civilizations on a time line and establishing their location in the world, students were surprised to discover that Egypt, Greece, and Rome shared the Mediterranean world and that India and China shared the Himalayan Mountains on their borders. The end result of this teacher's sociological approach to the teaching of history was the construction of a narrative of the ancient world, a common story that united Egypt, Greece, and Rome without marginalizing the civilizations of India and China. Perhaps more importantly, the students learned that history is about explaining and understanding social life, not about evaluating the "cultural worth" of civilizations.

Conclusions

Critics have complained that the introduction of multiple perspectives in the curriculum makes history radically relativistic. They argue that students will no longer be able to evaluate the merits of competing points of view about contentious historical events, such as the Holocaust, the Vietnam War, and the civil rights movement. If students study the social organization of the Upic, the Americans, and the Mexicans and learn that one cultural system is as functional as another, how, they ask, do students judge the superiority of any one society? Our response to this criticism is that the purpose of history is to explain, not to evaluate. When a multiperspectival history is taught well, it will provide students with the grounds on which they can understand the interactions, conflicts, and negotiations among diverse groups that constituted significant historical events. As Levine argues (1996, 160),

> It is crucial to study and understand as many of the contributing cultures and their interactions with one another as possible, not as a matter of "therapeutic" history, as the opponents of multiculturalism keep insisting, not to placate or flatter minority groups and make them feel good, as they also assert, but as a simple matter of *understanding* the nature and complexities of American culture and the processes by which it came, and continues to come, into being.

Revisionist and multicultural histories of the United States (Nash 1992; Zinn 1980; Takaki 1993) have created meaningfully inclusive narratives of U.S. history that embody the diversity of U.S. society, narratives that help students understand the subjectivities and actions of diverse groups and individuals as they interacted within a common history. Moreover, these histories provide students with a "record of what power has done" (Gitlin 1995, 20), a record that is found in the interactions between diverse groups. The history of power in the United States is essential in providing students with knowledge that does not detach the present from the historical process (Levine 1996, xv). Without a common historical narrative that embodies diversity, there is no usable past that represents for students racial conflict, discrimination, and injustice, whether these are understood as psychological or structural realities. As Banks argues (1997, 9), we need to provide students with a history that enables them to "acquire a comprehensive view of people of color and their interactions with mainstream groups" and that represents people of color as "shapers of their own destinies."

One important result of our sociological approach to the teaching of history is that it invites us to rethink the relationship between identity and society. Multicultural approaches—as they exist in practice in actual classrooms—begin with peoples' ethnic or racial identities, which relegates society to a residual status. We suggest beginning with society, which of necessity will turn our attention to how racial and ethnic identities are constituted in social life. Identity is not a fixed characteristic of individuals and groups. It is not always a relevant attribute that affects interactions in particular ways. Identity is instead a fluid process that emerges in interaction. Such features as race, ethnicity, and gender may be relevant in a variety of ways and may be relevant in some situations but not in others. Furthermore, the "identity politics" that emerge from multiculturalism celebrates membership in a racial, ethnic, or gendered group, which deflects attention away from the civic identities needed to maintain a democratic, civil society (Gitlin 1995).

The question to address, then, is not simply, What difference does cultural difference make? This approach can fall into the essentialist trap of assuming that race, ethnicity, and gender are ascribed—indeed, permanent characteristics of people. The question to address is, What differences make a difference in specific historical events and periods? This approach assumes that identities are fluid and ever changing, that they are achieved, constructed, contested, and constituted through social interaction. This sociological view of identity in relationship to society necessitates a different kind of work in the history classroom, the kind that we have tried to outline. In this approach, the relevance of diversity in history is always an empirical question, and the focus of attention is always on society, out of which identity emerges.

We accept the premise that the teaching of history requires a common narrative, but we believe that the common core of this narrative should be the struggle for civil rights, not the celebration of inevitable progress. We accept the critique that the historical narrative often taught in schools is Eurocentric, has excluded the voices of people of color and women, and has neglected or suppressed issues of injustice. We also recognize the complexity of the task of teaching history, that is, constructing and teaching a narrative that tells us who we are as Americans, while being inclusive and honest about institutional racism, exploitation, and discrimination.

If we begin the teaching of history with an inclusive narrative about the struggle for civil rights, students will draw on it unconsciously. The inclusive narrative will provide them "naturally" with a diverse view of what it means to be an American. When an inclusive narrative is the taken-for-granted starting point, issues concerning social justice, equality, and discrimination are accessible, because everyone is present, everyone is an active participant, and everyone is a speaker in the conversation about the constitution of American society.

WORKS CITED

Apple, Michael W., and J. A. Beane. 1995. *Democratic schools.* Alexandria, VA: Association for Supervision and Curriculum Development.

Aronowitz, Stanley, and Henry A. Giroux. 1985. *Education under siege: The conservative, liberal, and radical debate over schooling.* Hadley, MA: Bergin and Garvey.

Banks, James A. 1988. *Multiethnic education: Theory and practice.* Boston: Allyn and Bacon.

———. 1989. Multicultural education: Characteristics and goals. In *Multicultural Education: Issues and Perspectives,* ed. James A. Banks and Cherry A. McGee Banks, 2–26. Boston: Allyn and Bacon.

———. 1997. *Educating citizens in a multicultural society.* New York: Teachers College Press.

Banks, James A., and Cherry A. McGee Banks, eds. 1995. *Handbook of research on multicultural education.* New York: MacMillan.

Bennett, William J. 1992. *The De-valuing of America: The fight for our culture and our children.* New York: Summit.

Bloom, Allan. 1987. *The closing of the American mind: How higher education has failed democracy and impoverished the souls of today's students.* New York: Simon and Schuster.

Bush, George. 1991. *Goals 2000: An American educational strategy.* Washington, DC: United States Department of Education.

California State Department of Education. 1990. *Framework for history and social studies.* Sacramento: Department of Education.

Cheney, Lynne V. 1995. *Telling the truth: Why our culture and our country have stopped making sense—and what we can do about it.* New York: Simon and Schuster.

Cochran-Smith, Marilyn. 1995. Color blindness and basket making are not the answers: Confronting the dilemmas of race, culture, and language diversity in teacher education. *American Educational Research Journal* 32, no. 3:493–522.

Crabtree, Charlotte, and Gary B. Nash. 1994a. *National standards for United States history: Exploring the United States experience, grades 5–12.* Los Angeles: National Center for History in the Schools.

———. 1994b. *National standards for world history: Exploring the paths to the present, grades 5-12.* Los Angeles: National Center for History in the Schools.

———. 1996. *National standards for teaching history: Basic edition.* Los Angeles: National Center for History in the Schools.

Darder, Antonia. 1991. *Culture and power in the classroom: A critical foundation for education.* New York: Bergin and Garvey.

D'Souza, Dinesh. 1991. *Illiberal education: The politics of race and sex on campus.* New York: Free.

Dyer, Richard. 1997. *White.* New York: Routledge.

Erickson, Peter. 1991. Rather than reject a common culture, multiculturalism advocates a more complicated route by which to achieve it. *Chronicle of Higher Education* 37, no. 41 (June 26): B1–B3.

Finn, Chester. 1991. *We must take charge.* New York: Basic.

Gates, Henry Louis. 1995. Multiculturalism: A conversation among different voices. In *Rethinking schools,* ed. D. Levine, R. Lowe, B. Peterson, and R. Tenorio, 7–9. New York: New Press.

Giroux, Henry. 1992. *Border crossings: Cultural workers and the politics of education.* New York: Routledge.

Giroux, Henry, and Peter McLaren, eds. 1989. *Critical pedagogy, the state, and cultural struggle.* Albany: State University of New York Press.

———. 1994. *Between borders: Pedagogy and the politics of cultural studies.* New York: Routledge and Kegan Paul.

Gitlin, Todd. 1995. *The twilight of common dreams: Why America is wracked by culture wars.* New York: Henry Holt.

Hirsch, E. D., Jr. 1987. *Cultural literacy: What every American needs to know.* Boston: Houghton Mifflin.

Jackson, Sandra, and Jose Solis. 1995. *Beyond comfort zones in multiculturalism: Confronting the politics of privilege.* Westport, CT: Bergin and Garvey.

Kincheloe, Joe L., and Shirley R. Steinberg. 1997. *Changing multiculturalism.* Philadelphia: Open University Press.

Kincheloe, Joe L., Shirley R. Steinberg, Nelson M. Rodríguez, and Ronald E. Chennault. 1998. *White reign: Deploying whiteness in America.* New York: St. Martin's.

Ladson-Billings, G., and W. R. Tate. 1995. Toward a critical race theory of education. *Teachers College Record* 97, no. 1 (fall): 47–68.

Lesko, Nancy, and Leslie Rebecca Bloom. 1998. Close encounters: Truth, experience, and interpretation in multicultural teacher education. *Journal of Curriculum Studies* 30, no. 4:375–95.

Levine, L. W. 1996. *The opening of the American mind: Canons, culture, and history.* Boston: Beacon.

Lipsitz, George. 1998. *The possessive investment in whiteness: How white people profit from identity politics.* Philadelphia: Temple University Press.

Massaro, Toni Marie. 1993. *Constitutional literacy: A core curriculum for a multicultural nation.* Durham, NC: Duke University Press.

McCarthy, C. 1998. *The uses of culture: Education and the limits of ethnic affiliation.* New York: Routledge.

McCarthy, C., and W. Crichlow. 1993. *Race, identity, and representation in education.* New York: Routledge.

McCarthy, C., and A. I. Willis. 1995. The politics of culture: Multicultural education after the canon debate. In *Beyond comfort zones in multiculturalism: Confronting the politics of privilege,* ed. S. Jackson and J. Solis, 67–87 . Westport, CT: Bergin and Garvey.

McIntyre, Alice. 1997. *Making meaning of whiteness: Exploring racial identity with white teachers.* Albany: State University of New York Press.

McLaren, Peter L. 1991. Critical pedagogy, multiculturalism, and the politics of risk and resistance. *Journal of Education* 173, no. 3:109–39.

———. 1997. *Revolutionary multiculturalism: Pedagogies of dissent for the new millennium.* Boulder, CO: Westview.

Mehan, Hugh, Angela Lintz, Dina Okamoto, and John Wills. 1995. Ethnographic studies of multicultural education in classrooms and schools. In *Handbook of research on multicultural education,* ed. James A. Banks and Cherry A. McGee Banks, 129–44. New York: MacMillan.

Nash, Gary B. 1986. Thomas Peters: Millwright, soldier, and deliverer. In *Race, class, and politics: Essays on American colonial revolutionary society,* 269–82. Chicago: University of Illinois Press.

———. 1992. *Red, white, and black: The peoples of early North America.* Englewood Cliffs, NJ: Prentice Hall.

Nash, Gary B., Charlotte Crabtree, and Ross E. Dunn. 1997. *History on trial: Culture wars and the teaching of the past.* New York: Knopf.

Nieto, Sonia. 1992. *Affirming diversity: The sociopolitical context of multicultural education.* White Plains, NY: Longman.

Omi, Michael, and Howard Winant. 1993. On the theoretical concept of race. In *Race, identity, and representation in education,* ed. C. McCarthy and W. Crichlow, 3–10. New York: Routledge.

Ravitch, Diane. 1990. Multiculturalism: *E pluribus plures. Key Reporter* 56, no. 1:1–4.

Richter, Conrad. 1953. *The Light in the Forest.* New York: Knopf.

Schlesinger, Arthur M., Jr. 1992. *The disuniting of America.* New York: Norton.

Sleeter, Christine E. 1993. How white teachers construct race. In *Race, identity, and representation in education,* ed. C. McCarthy and W. Crichlow, 157–71. New York: Routledge.

Sleeter, Christine E., and Carl A. Grant. 1987. An analysis of multicultural education in the United States. *Harvard Education Review* 57, no. 4:421–44.

———. 1988. *Making choices for multicultural education: Five approaches to race, class, and gender.* Columbus, OH: Merrill.

———. 1991. Mapping terrains of power: Student knowledge versus classroom knowledge. In *Empowerment through multicultural education,* ed. C. E. Sleeter, 49–67. Albany: State University of New York Press.

Sleeter, Christine E., and Peter L. McLaren. 1995. *Multicultural education, critical pedagogy and the politics of difference.* Albany, NY: State University of New York Press.

Swidler, Ann. 1986. Culture in action: Symbols and strategies. *American Sociological Review* 51, no. 3:273–86.

Takaki, Ronald. 1993. *A different mirror: A history of multicultural America.* New York: Little, Brown.

Titone, Connie. 1998. *Educating the white teacher as ally.* In *White reign: Deploying whiteness in America,* ed. Joe L. Kincheloe, Shirley R. Steinberg, Nelson M. Rodríguez, and Ronald E. Chennault, 159–75. New York: St. Martin's.

Torres, Carlos Alberto. 1998. *Democracy, education, and multiculturalism.* Lanham, MD: Rowman and Littlefield.

Weil, Danny K. 1998. *Toward a critical multicultural literacy: Theory and practice for education for liberation.* New York: Peter Lang.

Wertsch, James V. 1998. *Mind as action.* New York: Oxford University Press.

Wills, John S. 1994. Popular culture, curriculum, and historical representation: The situation of Native Americans in American history and the perpetuation of stereotypes. *Journal of Narrative and Life History* 4, no. 4:277–94.

———. 1996. Who needs multicultural education? White students, U.S. History, and the construction of a usable past. *Anthropology and Education Quarterly* 27, no. 3:365–89.

Zinn, Howard. 1980. *A people's history of the United States.* New York: Harper Collins.

Chapter 3

From Freedom to Manners: African American Literacy in the Nineteenth Century

Tom Fox
California State University, Chico
Chico, CA

The most significant feature of research in composition studies in the last fifteen years has been the sustained attention paid to the ways that history has shaped the teaching of writing. Powerful and influential historical critiques by James Berlin (1984), Susan Miller (1991), and others have concentrated on the powerful role that Harvard's first composition course in the late nineteenth century played in shaping the pedagogy and curriculum in composition. These critiques have shown how Harvard's entrance exam, first-year course, and current-traditional pedagogy created an unsavory legacy of gatekeeping and social-stratifying functions for composition.

Not many scholars doubt that Harvard's course deeply influenced the ways that composition is organized and taught, yet concentrating on one elite university's writing program, no matter how influential, can inhibit the possible contributions of other, less visible histories. Susan Miller argues in *Textual Carnivals* (1991, 34) that in academic histories of composition, "actual writing" is "undiscoursed." In other words, nonacademic writing is excluded from formal histories of writing and rhetoric, and with few exceptions, the history of composition is only the history of institutionalized instruction.

Originally published as "From Freedom to Manners: African American Literary Instruction," *Forum* 6, no. 1 (winter 1995): 1–12. Reprinted with permission.

This historiographical exclusion may function politically to legitimate a particular view of writing and writing instruction, as well as a particular social and political agenda that helped form these institutionalized practices (Miller 1991, 34–35). The project of writing the "undiscoursed" history of composition may serve institutional instruction by extending our consciousness of writing instruction beyond the oppressive model provided by Harvard. For students and teachers in composition classes in today's universities and colleges, expansive histories of composition could provide promising models of teaching and learning, models that could attract and retain a broader range of our social strata, models that could shift the historically oppressive definition of composition originating at Harvard toward broader, more inclusive ones of literacy in general.

Writing, Freedom, and Repression

The history of literacy practices by African Americans in the nineteenth century is a particularly compelling story. Central to this history is the transformation of ideas of literacy from the time of slavery, where literacy was clearly identified with freedom for slaves, to the time of emancipation, where, tragically, those ideas were compromised in schools by instruction that emphasized manners and character. For today's teachers and students of composition, this complex history offers insight into the still compelling idea of literacy as a means of achieving freedom for African Americans and into the pattern of institutional domestication of literacy that works against that idea.

An obvious feature of African American literacy in the pre–Civil War South was that it was a transparently political and pragmatic means of achieving freedom. Despite threats of dismemberment (cutting off the index finger was a common punishment for slaves who were caught writing), whipping, and even death, African Americans learned to read and write in remarkable numbers. From 5 to 10 percent of slaves could read and write. Based on her extensive examination of a variety of sources, Janet Duitsman Cornelius, in her important book *When I Can Read My Title Clear* (1991), has argued that the 10 percent figure is more likely the accurate one.

That any significant population of slaves learned to read and write testifies to the strength and ingenuity of slave resistance, considering the violent opposition to slave literacy. In the 1830s, following various publicized slave rebellions, fearful white Southerners believed that literacy was a central cause of rebellion. As a result of this fear, they enacted legislation that made teaching and learning literacy illegal. South Carolina, which historically had banned slave literacy in 1740 and again in 1800, passed one of the most restrictive laws. The discussion that preceded its enactment in 1834 continually referred to the role that literacy played in the elaborately organized scheme for rebellion in Charleston—which had occurred eight years before—that had been planned by a literate slave, Denmark Vesey. Slave owner Whitemarsh Seabrook, whom Cornelius calls "fussy and somewhat pedantic," unrelentingly led the movement to ban literacy teaching to slaves. His tactics were to argue that literacy and religion were the two main threats to slave owners' power and were "most dangerous when combined" (Cornelius 1991, 40). During the years 1829 through 1834, Georgia, Louisiana, North Carolina, Virginia, Alabama, and South Carolina all passed antiliteracy laws. Most laws also included prohibitions to assemble.

While the legal suppression of literacy learning was difficult to enforce, antiliteracy laws were a symbolic gesture that signified the collective fear slave owners had about reading and writing, and they legitimated (for them) the violent means used to punish slaves for learning to read and write. These laws were perhaps aimed as much at Northern abolitionists, who wished to teach slaves to read and write, as they were at slaves. Brutal slaveholders, however, never needed laws to enforce their wishes. Cornelius (1991, 66) cites several stories of slaves who told of the punishments—from whipping, to amputating fingers to prevent writing, to hanging—for getting caught reading and writing. It was clear to any slave in the early nineteenth century that reading and writing were risks.

Apparently, slave owners had a reason to fear literacy. They cited the fact that strong leaders among slaves, from Nat Turner to Denmark Vesey in Charleston, saw printed texts—abolitionist texts, biblical texts, newspaper reports of slave rebellions—as "an inspiration for revolt" (Cornelius 1991, 30). As further evidence, they cited, in particular, David Walker's *Appeal in Four Articles* ([1848] 1969), a passionate and powerful exhortation to revolt.

Walker's text was especially troublesome to them. According to the "Brief Sketch of the Life and Character of David Walker" that accompanies the 1848 edition, the *Appeal* "caused more commotion among slaveholders than any volume of its size that was ever issued from an American press" (vi). It is not hard to see why. Walker's *Appeal* strikes at the heart of all slaveholder's fears. First of all, it was addressed to "Colored Citizens" (1969) and assumed a literate slave audience. This rhetorical move excluded white readers, placing the issues of freedom and liberty beyond their control. Walker repeatedly addressed his audience as "my beloved brethren," and he sometimes even more pointedly selected his audience: "Men of colour, who are also of sense, for you particularly is my appeal designed" (40). For the planters to imagine an audience of slaves, in the way that Walker demanded they imagine it, would be to destroy their image of slaves as subhuman. By way of brilliantly critiquing not the most racist planters but "moderate" arguments, such as Thomas Jefferson's section on slavery in *NOTES on the State of Virginia* and Henry Clay's plan for Liberian colonization, Walker repeatedly argued for open insurrection. His image of literacy was, I believe, representative.

> You have to prove to the Americans and the world, that we are MEN, and not *brutes* as we have been represented, and by millions treated. Remember, to let the aim of your labours among your brethren, and particularly the youths, be the dissemination of education and religion. . . . Some few of them, may make out to scribble tolerably well, over half a sheet of paper, which I believe has hitherto been a powerful obstacle in our way, to keep us from acquiring knowledge. (42)

This "knowledge," Walker made clear, is knowledge of the brutality of slavery, knowledge that will "make the tyrants quake and tremble" (44). Literacy has power, he argued, because slave owners will know that "their infernal deeds of cruelty will be made known to the world" (44). Additionally, Walker argued that once educated, slaves will no longer tolerate slave conditions.

> Do you suppose one man of good sense and learning would submit himself, his father, mother, wife and children, to be slaves to a wretched man like himself, who, instead of compensating him for his labours, chains, handcuffs and beats him and family almost to death, leaving life enough in them, however, to work for, and call him master? No! no! . . . The bare name of educating the coloured people, scares our cruel oppressors almost to death. (44)

Walker's rhetorical identification with slaves, his knowledge of history, his skills in argumentation, his unrelenting assertions of African American humanity and power, and the widespread dissemination of his pamphlet gave Southern planters good reason to fear literacy.

In the slave-owning South, the power structures, both legislative and social, seemed to understand this role that literacy could play in challenging oppression. While it is difficult to imagine in the 1990s (given the minimal and mechanical definitions of literacy today), literacy was at the very center of the debate about slavery in the 1830s. African American slaves and freedmen sought literacy as a means of challenging and transforming their communities and the nation. In doing so, they shook the ideological underpinnings of Southern slavery.

In the face of a threatened and determined opposition, slaves felt very powerful motives for writing. Many of these motives—if not most—were pragmatically political, but I will begin with one that may seem less immediately so. One of the means of political action was resisting the definitions of (in)humanity imposed on slaves by white society. As many commentators on literacy have pointed out, literacy in the Western world has been associated with humanity, the very quality of being a human. Racist beliefs defined slaves as subhuman, incapable of or unsuited to many intellectual tasks, not the least of which was literacy, and especially writing. Robert Stepto, in *From behind the Veil* (1979), argues that the reason many slave narratives had to be "authenticated" by white people was that their audience, while perfectly willing to believe slaves could be free, had difficulty believing slaves could write. Charles T. Davis and Henry Louis Gates, Jr., concur (1985, xv), arguing that the slave narrative "arose as a response to and a refutation of claims that slaves *could not* write." For a slave, the act of writing itself challenged the very ideological structure of slavery.

Writing also involved an assertion of a collective identity, which the removal from Africa, the separation of families, and the various laws that prevented assembly (many of which accompanied antiliteracy laws) made urgent. Paradoxically, opposition to the very humanity of slaves made writing more urgently important. Davis and Gates write (1985, xxiii):

> The slave narrative represents the attempts of blacks to *write themselves into being*. What a curious idea: through the mastery of formal Western languages, the presupposition went, a black person

> could become a human being by an act of self-creation through the mastery of language. Accused of having no collective history by Hegel in 1813, blacks responded by publishing hundreds of individual histories.

Literacy—especially writing—carried with it this oppositional stance. For instance, the fact that Frederick Douglass's master opposed his learning to read and write made Douglass all the more determined to become literate. In fact, he allows some credit to the opposition of his master: "In learning to read, therefore, I am not sure that I owe as much to the opposition of my master as to the kindly assistance of my mistress" (quoted in Cornelius 1991, 1). Thomas Webber, in *Deep Like the Rivers* (1978, 135), claims that "the efforts of the white community to discourage the learning attempts of their slaves only strengthened the slaves' resolve." He cites the experience of Austin Steward as representative; after he was flogged for studying a book, Steward reported:

> [I]nstead of giving me the least idea of giving it up, [the flogging] only made me look upon it [i.e., reading] as a more valuable attainment. Else, why should my oppressor feel so unwilling that their slaves should possess that which they thought so essential to themselves? (Quoted in Webber 1978, 135)

Literacy was an individual and collective argument against the various, increasingly absurd defenses of slavery in the early nineteenth century. The assertion of collective identity was not as much a psychological act as it was a political act against slavery.

Most of the reasons that African Americans claimed for learning to read and write were pragmatic. Writing, in particular, was linked with freedom in the form of a pass. In a society so entrenched in the belief that slaves could not write, a slave could write himself a "pass" that would either allow him mobility or facilitate his escape. Although Frederick Douglass's autobiography offers the most famous example of a slave writing his own pass, many other slave narratives tell similar tales. Passes could be used to gain time to escape to the North or, as Cornelius notes, to gain temporary freedom to visit family members in other locations.

Writing became identified with freedom on this individual level, but it also became a part of the collective struggle, as the pamphlets of

Walker and others show. African Americans wrote—and read—to be involved with the ongoing struggle for collective freedom. This first protest literature took many forms: political pamphlets, slave narratives, court petitions for emancipation, and written accounts of slave rebellions. For both the slave populations and white slaveholders, the volume and force of this literature tied literacy with resistance.

This brief account of literacy learning among African Americans in slavery is in dramatic contrast to the institutional history of composition. Chronologically, the pre–Civil War period predates most common public schools, the sense of nationalism that was a consequence of the Civil War, and the linguistic standardization of the second half of the century. The context of African Americans' literacy—the fact that it worked against and outside dominant institutions—gave it a particular stamp of urgency, action, and, perhaps, political effectiveness.

Emancipation and the Domestication of Literacy

Some white Southerners saw the unbridled, extrainstitutional nature of African American literacy as its most dangerous feature. Instead of arguing for antiliteracy laws, which they perceived would be ineffective (and they perceived correctly, since literacy learning had gone on outside the purview of repressive masters), many white Southerners argued that the best way to preserve slavery would be to institutionalize literacy. In fact, in the public discussions preceding South Carolina's antiliteracy laws, some Southern whites argued that formal schooling for slaves would better control the content of their learning and make slaves more submissive, industrious, and accepting (Cornelius 1991, 45–46).

Regardless of Southern whites' wishes, institutionalized schooling and literacy instruction came soon enough. As soon as Northern armies began to conquer Southern lands, slaves were set free. And as soon as slaves were set free, a wide variety of people with vastly different sets of purposes began to set up schools. Ultimately, these schools were governed by a federal agency, the Freedmen's Bureau. The Freedmen's Bureau was originally created to deal with freed slaves' immediate needs, such as food, shelter, and health. Within a year of its creation, the Freedmen's Bureau concentrated on education, to the exclusion of other, more urgent political issues (e.g., land and franchise). This sole concentration on education as the one means to equality deserves scrutiny. Most scholars of education, with the notable exception of Ronald Butchart in *Northern Schools, Southern Blacks, and Reconstruction* (1980), see the activities of the Freedmen's Bureau as anomalous in U.S. history as a whole, where there has otherwise been persistent neglect or antagonism toward African American education. They note that the schools of the Freedmen's Bureau brought over twenty-five hundred teachers (many of them Northern white women) to the South to teach newly enfranchised slaves (Butchart 1980, 4). As the first system of institutionalized instruction in literacy to African Americans in this country, the schools of the Freedmen's Bureau altered both the symbolic role and the actual role that literacy had played in the lives of African Americans.

In the pre–Civil War time, literacy for African Americans symbolized freedom by contradicting the dominant class's definition of Africans as subhuman. Once emancipated, freedmen retained these ideas about literacy. They attended the schools of the Freedmen's Bureau in droves and at great sacrifice. Teachers were faced with class sizes from fifty to one hundred, and many children and adults were turned away. Teacher after teacher remarked on the seriousness of their students. Butchart writes (1980, 170): "The intense desire for knowledge and literacy was reflected in the classroom. Teachers and observers marveled at the freedmen's zealous application to schoolwork, rapid advancement, and evidence of mental equality with whites." Northern teachers, steeped in the same racist ideologies as the South, were particularly astonished to find ex-slaves already reading and writing. James Anderson (1988, 5) sees this fact as evidence of the "former slaves' fundamental belief in the value of literate culture" and their determination "to secure schooling for themselves and their children."

The motives for attending the schools of the Freedmen's Bureau were much the same as motives for learning literacy before emancipation. Freedmen went to school to achieve practical power. It was as much a part of the collective movement for freedom after slavery as it had been before. Ex-slaves learned to read and write so that they could read their employment contracts and, for the lucky, the papers that allowed them to own property; so that they could participate in a newly opened political process; and so that they could foster collective racial pride. Ex-slaves also retained the ideological and symbolic understanding of literacy from days of enslavement. In the words of James Anderson (1988, 17), "emancipation extruded an ex-slave class with a fundamentally different consciousness of literacy [from whites], a class that viewed reading and writing as a contradiction of oppression."

Ultimately, both the practical political ends of education and the ideological hope for equality through education were betrayed in the years after the Civil War. Neither the planters in the South nor the Northern reformers had ideas for schools that would have met ex-slaves' political needs. Schools were central to the Freedmen's Bureau; after a year of its existence, schools were just about all that the Freedmen's Bureau was engaged in. Reconstruction had promised land reform and a fundamental redistribution of wealth. It had promised real opportunity. In the years shortly after the war, one by one, the bureau and the nation—and the Southern planters who regained their dominance—turned their backs on real reforms, leaving only schooling. Butchart (1980, 9) is most succinct on this point.

> The Afro-Americans were on the threshold of freedom. They needed land, protection, and a stake in society. They needed and demanded meaningful power. They were given instead a school. The gift was vastly inadequate to the needs of men and women set free in a vengeful, vindictive society. Indeed, as the school fell under the control of a race and a class with interests opposed to those of southern blacks, education was not merely inadequate, it was utterly inappropriate.

As the Freedmen's Bureau became more and more concerned with schools, and as it took control of even the schools run by blacks, literacy instruction for ex-slaves switched from literacy for liberation to literacy for social control. Curricular materials from the schools of the Freedmen's Bureau clearly show stress on manners and individual industry. While capitalizing on motives for demonstrating "humanity" and achieving economic freedom, the texts for freedmen represent literacy in a fundamentally different and conflicting light from the image of literacy as liberating. Some of the schools used the same textbooks as in white schools, while others used materials specifically created for Freedmen's schools. These materials, as would be expected, varied according to the ideological leanings of the groups who published and used them. Since many of the Freedmen's schools were founded by evangelical aid societies, the readers reflected religious values of temperance, piety, and domesticity. In most cases, very few texts addressed the conditions of slaves or the conditions of freedom. The more conservative books, those published by the American Tract Society (ATS), did address slavery and freedom, but they avoided all criticism of planters and presented the freedmen in demeaning ways—as lazy, unkempt, docile, dependent, or mentally inferior, and always in the role of an agricultural laborer. Prior to the war, the ATS published numerous religious tracts, but in no way could the organization be considered antislavery. Its materials reflected its opposition to black equality.

The ATS readers stand out in contrast to another choice for freedmen, Lydia Maria Child's *The Freedmen's Book* ([1865] 1968). In many ways, Child's book extends the ideology of literacy that the slaves held prior to the war. Child's story "The Meeting in the Swamp," for instance, draws on the ways that collectivity and literacy served liberation. It is the story of a slave owner, Mr. Duncan, who follows a slave to a secret meeting. There he witnesses a man who proclaims, "at last I finds out how de white man always git he foot on de black man" (108). His answer is literacy, and he holds up the newspaper to show it. The man describes learning to read by tricking his master's son; he describes using reading to inform himself and his fellow slaves about possible political developments that pertain to their freedom.

More than other readers, Child's selections (most written by herself) openly criticize slaveholders. In "The Beginning and Progress of Emancipation in the British West Indies," Child takes particular aim at the fact that West Indian slave owners kept their slaves "in brutal ignorance" (128). She ridicules the response of the slave owners to missionaries intent on teaching Bible literacy: "They said if slaves were instructed they would rise in rebellion against their masters. The English people replied that it must be a very bad system which made it dangerous for human beings to read the Bible" (128). Additionally, in her biographies of Madison Washington and Frederick Douglass, Child represents literacy learning as, in part, an act of rebellion.

Certainly, by the very fact of her inclusions of writings by Francis W. Harper, Frederick Douglass, Phillis Wheatley, and other African Americans, and by the fact that her text more openly represents the cruelty of slave owners and the resistance of slaves through literacy, Child's text differs from both McGuffey's readers—which were used throughout the schools of the Freedmen's Bureau—and the more conservative texts from ATS. Yet *The Freedmen's Book* also represents literacy learning as more domesticating than liberating. In the final essay,

"Advice from an Old Friend," Child stresses the power of individual character as a means of political reform. She claims that her biographies of black revolutionaries "prove that the power of *character* can overcome all external disadvantages, even that most crushing of disadvantages, Slavery" (269). The content of this character prevents the kinds of critical incisiveness or collective action that would have served the freedmen's political needs at the time. Child's essay argues for unsurprising features of character and claims the validity of these features by referring to the biographies of black revolutionaries that Child herself wrote. She argues that for emancipation to be successful, the ex-slaves needed to be "sober, industrious, and honest" (269). She devotes paragraphs to the virtues of manners, personal appearance, and thriftiness. While these characteristics veer significantly from the pragmatic education of the slaves, they are couched in similar political frames. After informing her readers that slavery remains legal in other countries, Child relates the following lesson on the virtues of tidy homes:

> . . . if your homes look neat, and your clothes are clean and whole, and your gardens well weeded, and your work faithfully done, whether for yourselves or others, then all the world will cry out, "You see that negroes *can* take care of themselves; and it is a sin and a shame to keep such men in Slavery." (270)

In addition to being insufficient political advice, the use of this statement in a pedagogical context sets up a sharply divided sense of literacy, one originating in slavery and building on a real and symbolic connection with liberation, yet one that also misuses that connection by displacing the tremendous political needs of the ex-slaves for political power in the domain of individual manners.

Obviously, the curriculum is not the same as the education. There is no evidence that the ex-slaves took Child's advice and traded in political action for planter boxes in front of their homes. Indeed, most of the evidence suggests a great deal of resistance to white teachers in general. Anderson's history of black education is the most thorough on this point. Even before the establishment of the Freedmen's Bureau, ex-slaves had set up schools for themselves. Thomas Alvord, superintendent of schools for the Freedmen's Bureau, found a whole system of black-initiated, black-run schools. Sociologists W. E. B. Du Bois, Carter Woodson, and others all point to this system as the foundation of public education in the South. The freedmen showed a clear preference for black teachers, sometimes offending Northern teachers. This preference stemmed not only from deep mistrust of whites but also from a desire to resist "external control" and, according to Anderson (1988, 12), to test "their capacity to restructure their lives, to establish their freedom."

For Northerners as well as for Southerners, the Civil War and the potential political and social enfranchisement of the freedmen broke open the world. Reconstruction promised a radically new political and social system. Literacy for African Americans was a part of this new society, though it was by no means as important for political transformation as were landownership or voting rights. Yet the remarkable—perhaps unprecedented—commitment to schooling reflected a continued belief that literacy had the power to "help raise the freed people to an appreciation of their historic responsibility to build a better society" and that "any significant reorganization of the southern political economy was indissolubly linked to their education in the principles, duties, and obligations appropriate to a democratic social order" (Anderson 1988, 28).

Once institutional writing instruction was made available to ex-slaves—and made available with rhetoric that drew on established notions about the connections between freedom and literacy—schools betrayed the rhetoric of emancipation through the curriculum and pedagogy of character and manners. The social agenda became selection, indoctrination, and gatekeeping. "Emancipation" changed from a politically pragmatic process of writing to a once-removed process of admission and acculturation. The standards of admission and acculturation were (and in many respects remain) a driving force that more often reproduced the academic manners of the elite. These standards evolved into standards that delineated racial and linguistic boundaries based on culture.

Conclusion

The literacy history of African Americans in the nineteenth century, like the literacy of most any group, is a complicated mix of hope and despair. The utility of this history to composition teachers is not self-evident. I hope that with more inclusive histories, we can begin to see more urgently our responsibility for creating more inclusive institutions. The continuing critique of institutionalized teaching of writing is far from completed, and the troubling exclusion of African Americans from higher education continues. Applied to the schools of the Freedmen's Bureau, this critique shows us, with historical depth, the ways that formal literacy education has, for the most part, failed to generate social or political power for African Americans. Additionally, the stories of the heroic commitment to literacy during slavery and after prevent the easy dismissal of school failure by arguing that African Americans live in an "oral culture," or in a culture that does not support education. Legitimating these histories in academic classrooms and journals is of important consequence to teachers and students of composition.

This history is of special importance to African American students in composition studies or those considering composition studies. If we imagine the history of African American literacy as already a part of composition's past, the institutional context for composition becomes richer and more relevant to African Americans, providing them with both new opportunities to locate critiques of literacy instruction and new opportunities to forge continuities with earlier African Americans' remarkable uses of literacy for freedom.

WORKS CITED

Anderson, James. 1988. *The education of blacks in the South, 1860–1935.* Chapel Hill: University of North Carolina Press.

Berlin, James. 1984. *Writing instruction in nineteenth-century colleges.* Carbondale: Southern Illinois University Press.

Butchart, Ronald E. 1980. *Northern schools, Southern blacks, and Reconstruction: Freedmen's education, 1862–1875.* Westport, CT: Greenwood.

Child, Lydia Maria. [1865] 1968. *The Freedmen's book.* Reprint, New York: Arno.

Cornelius, Janet Duitsman. 1991. *When I can read my title clear.* Columbia: University of South Carolina Press.

Davis, Charles T., and Henry Louis Gates, Jr. 1985. *The slave's narrative.* New York: Oxford.

Miller, Susan. 1991. *Textual carnivals.* Carbondale: Southern Illinois University Press.

Stepto, Robert. 1979. *From behind the veil.* Urbana: University of Illinois Press.

Walker, David. [1848] 1969. *Appeal in four articles.* Reprint, New York: Arno.

Webber, Thomas L. 1978. *Deep like the rivers.* New York: Norton.

Chapter 4

The View from Here: Toward a Critical Pedagogy in the Multiethnic Classroom

Gail Pérez
University of San Diego
San Diego, CA

So these are not essays as much as they are poems and
these are not poems as much as they are essays.
—Cheríe Moraga, *Loving in the War Years*

Professor Evelyn Hu-DeHart once commented (1993) that ethnic studies classes should not be "sensitivity training." My own experience with teaching at a small, fairly homogeneous college confirms her point that teachers of such classes are often perceived to be teaching "awareness" and not important literature, culture, history, and epistemology. Women faculty and faculty of color are often given this human relations task, a kind of time-consuming and unpaid labor that is often viewed in a negative light when tenure review comes around. Furthermore, as Malcolm X pointed out long ago, this labor actually belongs to the white community, since racism and other forms of discrimination begin there. But the fact remains that teaching matters of race, class, and gender does elicit powerful and contradictory feelings in our students. And if we are honest about the history of ethnic and women's studies, we would have to acknowledge that "awareness" has its roots in the idea of consciousness raising. Professional scholars have to ask whether or not they are willing to give up addressing consciousness, which so often serves as a prelude to activism. Much as I admire rigorous scholarship, I am going to argue that we should not ignore the activist origins of ethnic and women's studies, for several reasons: we would have to objectify the communities that produce so much of what we study (from rap to discos); we would have to ignore the standpoints of our diverse students; and we would endanger the continuation of our disciplines, because, as Patricia Hill Collins argues (1991), it is particularly the members of underrepresented groups who have the will to develop this scholarship on the basis of questions generated by lived experience. The question of activism necessarily leads us to questions of pedagogy, and it is this connection that I will attempt to explore here.

I realize that mine is a perilous argument to make at this historical moment, when Adela de la Torre can argue (1996) that so many programs "lack rigor" and that serious scholars are under attack by activist professors issuing the "litmus test" of authenticity. Unfortunately, de la Torre perpetuates a false dichotomy between activism and scholarship that trivializes the civil rights movement as being about rhetoric and culture (or gender) essentialisms. Her advice to "mainstream" ethnic studies reveals a deep misunderstanding of the educational reform of the 1960s, which was in fact to transform the university and not simply seek a space within its existing disciplines. Despite de la Torre's wish for the cultural capital that mainstreaming brings to any program, institutionalization will continue to be contested because of the very nature of ethnic studies. Ethnic studies and gender studies base their very existence on critiquing the claims of universalism and objectivity and on praxis. Hu-DeHart, in "The History, Development, and Future of Ethnic Studies" (1993), asks, "when would the total retreat of ethnic studies into the academy not be a contradiction?" Scholars like E. San Juan and Henry Louis Gates, she notes, wish to integrate the "academic goal of Ethnic Studies—the production of knowledge—with its original commitment to liberating and empowering the communities of color" (54). Her question "[H]ow could the field separate itself from the ongoing, real-life struggles of people of color?" is clearly rhetorical. Therefore, the battle for "the soul of ethnic studies" is not between sixties ideologues and serious scholars but between those who insist on the empowerment of communities of color and students, as well as on the validity of the epistemologies of marginalized people, and those who do not.

The question of diverse epistemologies is vexed but essential to questions of pedagogy. In American ethnic studies, the debate over knowledge is not simply a challenge to "Western" thought (although Afrocentric and indigenous perspectives might be viewed as such). It is also a consideration of how marginalized groups within U.S. culture have been excluded from the production of knowledge and, thus, how what "we" know is subject to revision as new information and new groups begin to enter the conversation. Indeed, the main epistemological contribution of ethnic studies is to assert that no one group has theorized reality; we must begin to look at social relations and culture from the vantage point of the marginalized. Once we include marginalized interpreters of the American scene, we must be willing to include sources of knowledge, such as oral history and popular culture, that have been previously ignored. Furthermore, as Patricia Hill Collins makes clear in *Black Feminist Thought* (1991), once we begin with the lived experience of marginalized groups, it becomes clear that knowledge is always produced in various sites and that universalism tends to obscure the situatedness and interestedness of its own claims. For this reason, ethnic and women's studies have always emphasized praxis.

> Black Women's concrete experiences as members of specific race, class, and gender groups as well as our concrete historical situations necessarily play significant roles in our perspectives on the world. No standpoint is neutral because no individual or group remains unembedded in the world. (Collins 1991, 33)

Hill's formulation further breaks down the dichotomy between theory and praxis, because such scholarship tends to be generated by the continuing lived struggles of the group: "The struggle for a self-defined Afrocentric feminist consciousness occurs through a merger of thought and action" (28). She also comments that, inevitably, the suppression of alternative epistemologies occurs because "a self-defined standpoint can stimulate resistance" in addition to creating an alternative "group valuation" through "an alternative consciousness" (26).

As a teacher of writing and American ethnic literature, I have used Hill's complex formulation of standpoint epistemology, praxis, and valorization of alternative consciousnesses to help me understand some of my own pedagogical impulses. Engaging these texts in a way that did not violate their often penetrating critique of education and knowledge frequently meant digging into critical pedagogy and experiential learning theory. Because the literature often revealed an ongoing struggle simply invisible to many students, it also seemed only natural to send them out into the community to experience the barrios, churches, and women's centers for themselves. I needed to uncover the theoretical foundation of these pedagogical impulses, the theory that refused to separate thought, praxis, alternative cultural practices, and community. By going out into the community, as I had encouraged my students to do, I found the answer close at hand, in the nearly simultaneous development of the Chicano studies and women's studies programs at San Diego State University. Both programs espoused the critical pedagogy associated with Paulo Freire, and both demanded that their programs link up with the community. It is especially important to go back to these roots now, when community service learning, "a community of writers," and the professionalization of ethnic and women's studies are in the air. All derived from social movements that, for all their flaws, raised questions about defining community, ethnicity, and empowerment that have not yet been resolved. Whether these terms are defined by those within institutions and corporations or by those whom these bodies are meant to "serve" will make a crucial difference in our teaching and in our lives. Indeed, what Ian Haney López calls "community ties" (and not race alone) are the main reasons to seek a diverse faculty and student body. In López's view, it is unquestionably community ties that bring new questions and perspectives into the scholarly world. Racial diversity is, for him, "the presence of people with significant and self-consciously held ties to the minority communities of their origins" (1993, 103).

This discussion, then, will fall into three divisions. First, I will explore the historical links between what we now call critical pedagogy and ethnic studies. Next, I will argue for the need to reconsider pedagogy when teaching ethnic texts. This is absolutely critical, because literacy is both a major "moment" in ethnic literature and a struggle for empowerment enacted every day in class. We must avoid the paradox of teaching the literature of people who are themselves excluded from school, of textualizing ethnicity to relieve ourselves of this contradiction—a contradiction that becomes nearly unbearable when we teach the vernacular texts of Tomás Rivera or Zora Neale Hurston while continuing to stigmatize speakers of the vernacular. The ethnic studies classroom must also be a site where who has "the word" and who has to hear it changes. In this regard, Linda Brodkey's (1996) insistence that literacy is writing and not simply reading is salutary, since it is as writers that we achieve social and institutional agency as "writers of the world" (23).

Finally, I will propose developmental models for using exploratory and more formal assignments to accomplish three ends: (1) to help students discover their own assumptions and view their responses to the texts as an ongoing process; (2) to encourage students to develop voice(s), especially within the institutional setting of the school; and (3) to develop writing assignments that have an experiential base. This last point respects the vibrant communities we read about, but it also refers to the importance of students' engaging with these communities. This is not simply an exaltation of popular knowledge; it is to understand that the living experience each of us has is, as Paulo Freire wrote (1995, 84), "the point of departure for the knowledge [we] create of the world." He continued, "'Their' world, in the last analysis, is the primary and inescapable face of the world itself."

Certainly, Paulo Freire's thought informs the educational reform movement of the 1960s and 1970s, especially in regard to ethnic studies. Reviewing this history reminds us that his pedagogy was created as anticolonial practice. Henry Giroux (1993, 177) laments the academic appropriation of Freire's *Pedagogy of the Oppressed* (1970) by the "insipid and dreary demands for pedagogical recipes dressed up in the jargon of abstracted progressive labels." Such appropriations, of course, obscure race and ethnicity, just as some definitions of multiculturalism erase discussion of decolonization. I essentially agree with M. Annette Jaimes Guerrero (1996, 50), who insists that "decolonization must take place before a genuine multiculturalism is established."

Thus, if we are willing to unpack the web of contradictions revealed by the presence of ethnic texts in our schools, teaching these texts can transform educational setting and practice. Transformation is the most important and enduring pedagogical concept of the past twenty-five years. It integrates into one complex process so many of the concepts presented in the rest of this chapter, and thus it deserves definition. As Alfred Alschuler (1980, 71) interprets Freire, transforming the world means "changing any part of external reality—erecting buildings, creating organizations, changing roles, rules, policies—in contrast with changing feelings, ideas, attitudes, beliefs, and prejudices." This explains why so many ethnic studies teachers are often impatient with the "facilitator" role (necessary as that role might be). Decolonizing means concretely changing existing institutions; it means using language in a special way that names the oppression in a context of dialogue. Transformation also includes the changing of subjectivities, especially in two ways: (1) as bell hooks says (1994, 187), we must understand that "it is first the potential oppressor within that we must resist, the potential victim within that we must rescue—otherwise we cannot hope for an end to domination"; and (2) we must be responsible for the ways in which we collude with oppressive situations. In other words, the pedagogy for ethnic studies has been historically linked to a notion of education that demands both inner and outer change (not one or the other). As should be clear from what follows, this is so because the presence of ethnic texts was preceded by the presence of ethnic bodies; the integration of schools preceded the flowering of ethnic literature, for obvious reasons.

Historical Background

Writing this chapter has allowed me to explore the culturally rich San Diego/Tijuana area in the way that I encourage my students to do. I wanted to explore the roots of ethnic and women's studies and critical pedagogy in the movement at San Diego State University. As previously noted, San Diego State University was the site of the first women's studies program in the country (1970) and the first Chicano studies department. This fact is generally obscured in the historical accounts. As early as 1968, Chicanos took over the administration building, demanding a Chicano Studies Center that would provide community and student services, as well as academic programs. Recruitment, counseling, a kitchen, a Barrio Station, and a press were all envisioned. As one of the founders, the noted Chicano poet Alurista (1994), explained, the changes were spearheaded by students and a few committed faculty. Students also drew support from community leaders; their efforts coincided with the creation of a community clinic, the Centro Cultural de la Raza, and the takeover of Chicano Park. As Alurista noted, the burden of social and educational change was not being placed on students alone; they had significant community support. This emphasis is reiterated in the key document to emerge from the Chicano student movement, the *Plan de Santa Barbara,* which clearly states the relationship of education to community: "The colleges and universities in the past have existed in an aura of omnipotence and infallibility. It is time that they be made responsible and responsive to the communities in which they are located or whose members they serve" (quoted in Muñoz 1989, 201).

My interviews with activists, such as Joyce and Leon Nower (1994) and Carla Kirkwood (1994), confirmed that women's and ethnic studies were distinguished from other programs by their insistence on being responsive to their constituencies. The Nowers helped found both a women's studies program and a black studies program. Joyce Nower pointed out that the women's studies program was modeled on the organizational model of the Chicano studies program: the academic program would be housed under a larger organization—the Center for Women's Studies—that would include community outreach, a storefront, child care, and so on. As with the Chicano studies program, the community wing of the women's studies program later left or was forced off campus. This defeated the core of the founders' radical pedagogy; as Leon Nower commented, "How good can an education be without community?" He made the recurrent point that these programs were special—they were to transform education in the entire university.

The power struggle within the women's studies program became legendary, resulting in a collective board (with significant student power) running the program until 1974. According to the student activist publication *Inside the Beast*, the struggle was over which model the program would follow. One kind of program is initiated by some combination of faculty and administration and emphasizes professionalism and the credibility of women's studies as a discipline. Such programs often exist on foundational support. The radical women preferred a second model that was closer to the movement, was student-based, and had, in this case, a socialist analysis that included race, class, and heterosexism. Obviously, the interaction between politics and the academy is still important to ethnic and women's studies (and increasingly to writing programs).

While some of the students came to feel that maintaining the program within the university bureaucracy was a waste of time and went off to organize in the workforce, they did, along the way, produce some excellent analyses. Because they had real power, their writing and their community work were on a high level. Their critique of middle-class feminism predicted the issues that filled the journals in the 1970s and 1980s: In what way were "all men" the enemy? How might an emphasis on psychological oppression turn off working-class women? Who is the community, and what kind of outreach is democratic? They came to the inevitable conclusion that examining one kind of oppression must expose other kinds, so they attempted to form coalitions on campus.

They protested the loss of activism on campus as the movement wound down: "Although we had an implied politics, our practice did not reflect our theory; we were not dealing with our own race, class, and heterosexual bias" (Kirkwood 1994). In retrospect, many aspects of this power struggle were destructive, but teachers must be impressed by the work of students who had actual power. We might learn from the fact that the most divisive issues seemed to be acceptance of foundation money and questions concerning just who the community is and who best represents it. These questions continue to be relevant in attempts to institute community-based learning. Such strife, as Joyce Nower's notes from the 1970s struggle reveal, plays into the hands of "opportunists" and the "chronically uncommitted, whom it absolves from getting down to work."

As both Carla Kirkwood and Alurista recall (both 1994), students also taught classes. They asked fundamental questions about knowledge and power. By feeding students into United Farm Workers picket lines, they relocated the site where knowledge is presumed to exist. By bringing members of the community into classes as "auditors," they demanded a reconsideration of who is receiving knowledge. By insisting on an interaction between theory and action, they insisted on praxis; one must act and reflect. One often feels today that "reflection" has become debased in the world of experiential education to refer to "processing feelings." In Freire's model, it has more to do with understanding the power relations that produce "reality" and transforming them. In this sense, the role of community is not an afterthought on campus but must be the starting point for any education that is liberatory and not simply adaptive.

The comments of teachers/activists in both movements emphasize that (at least ideally) a radical pedagogy means empowering the community, as well as the students and teachers. A glance at an often excellent text on service learning, *Praxis III: Voices in Dialogue,* shows that the pedagogy of the oppressed is pretty much reserved for oppressed students and classroom dynamics. One contributor writes, "The other premise of Freirian pedagogy is to empower students to realize that there is a different way to learn, and that Project Community is a space where this can happen" (Galura et al. 1995, 220). While a book like *Praxis* is imbued with Freire, the community remains an inarticulate other, and the subject position of students as both educators and educated is not adequately conceptualized. Students who do not come from the communities they serve must have revealed not only their oppression but also their privilege. The need to market service learning to universities keeps the focus on students, but this very focus perpetuates the institutions and not community development and outcomes. Writing from an African American perspective on Freire, bell hooks (1994, 54) redefines reciprocal help.

> Authentic help means that all who are involved help each other mutually, growing together in the common effort to understand the reality they seek to transform. Only through such praxis—in which those who help and those who are being helped help each other simultaneously—can the act of helping become free from the distortion in which the helper dominates the helped.

Programs that actually empower the community, not selected individuals, will become political. The movements at San Diego State were intent on creating critical consciousness in partnership with various community leaders. Leadership training in the 1990s has also raised questions about which community leaders should work in partnership with student leaders; this relationship is crucial in generating respect for those who work for change outside the academy.

As Paul Lauter and Florence Howe made clear in their fascinating *The Conspiracy of the Young* (1970), the Mississippi Freedom schools most closely approximated the educational ideal of students working to create community leaders who would then further specific community goals—in this case, voter registration and literacy. Mississippi Freedom classes also generated the crucial questions about identity and history that we associate with the growth of ethnic studies: "[The students'] need for identity and activity was organically one with the need for facts. It had to do with what happens when an individual begins to know himself as a part of history, with a past and a potential future as well as a present" (Lauter and Howe 1970, 41). The 1964 summer project was the product of young African American activists from the SNCC (Student Nonviolent Coordinating Committee) and CORE (Congress of Racial Equality) and offered its own "developmental" model for creating critical consciousness: students should begin by comparing their reality to that of others; they should understand how discrepancies in wealth and power are systematically created, explore value differences in a unit called "material *vs* soul things" (Lauter and Howe 1970, 41), and, finally, be introduced to social action in the movement. Here, the goals of ethnic content, radical pedagogy, and community action are woven into an organic whole. While ethnic studies, literacy, and community service learning are now bureaucracies and academic industries (often funded by foundations), they once coincided with decidedly grassroots movements. The simpler days might be gone, but the struggle to make all these educational offices responsive to community self-determination is not. Each is easily co-opted into the knowledge industry as a new brand of cutting-edge research or pedagogy.

Community service learning, promoted, for example, by the California branch of Campus Compact, an organization of college and university presidents, is a recent phenomenon that dwarfs the vision of kitchens and voting from twenty-five years ago. Since its goals "to engage higher education in its societal responsibilities" and "prepare students for lives as informed participants in a democracy" are unfocused, it especially needs to answer the pertinent questions asked long ago. Lauter and Howe (1970, 5–7) preferred the term *service for change* and defined it as an activity that does not preserve institutions but transforms them by implementing the self-determination of the groups served. For Lauter and Howe, the old idea of service (very much alive in the 1990s) was represented by the statement of the National Service Secretariat (1968):

> National service as a concept embraces the belief that an opportunity should be given every young person to serve his country in a manner consistent with the needs of the nation—recognizing national defense as the first priority—and consistent with the education and interests of those participating, without infringing on the personal or economic welfare of others but contributing to the liberty and well-being of all. (quoted in Lauter and Howe 1970, 6)

This should be compared to a counterinstitution founded by youth, called Vocations for Social Change. Their decidedly different emphasis is expressed in a 1968 newsletter cited by Lauter and Howe.

> Vocations for Social Change is based on two great hopes. We feel that there is a great need for institutional change in this country so that ordinary citizens can have greater control over the forces that limit their lives. . . . At the same time, we are greatly concerned

> about the quality of our lives and the lives of our fellow citizens. We want our work to produce change in the society and we also want it to provide meaning for us. (1970, 6)

While national service (chiefly represented by the Peace Corps and VISTA [Volunteers in Service to America]) no longer has the threat of the draft behind it, its ideology still potentially contradicts the social change demanded by certain grassroots movements. We must still ask in what sense the agencies to which we link students give them meaningless work or continue to make an often tacit appeal to volunteerism. The very notion of volunteering is class-bound, appealing to "those lineal descendants of the bearers of the service ethic whose self-definition is posed in terms of work and stewardship" (Lauter and Howe 1970, 334). Ethnic and working-class students immediately understand the class nature of service (VISTA and the Peace Corps found few recruits among them), and service work for women is also loaded. In addition, working for underfunded or poorly run agencies teaches negative lessons. If social justice is so important, why do we send unskilled young people at no or minimum wage to tackle the most serious social problems? Teachers or students who point out this contradiction will inevitably go beyond the vague rhetoric of Campus Compact and will no doubt be labeled as "biased" or "activist."

As Lauter and Howe state, the black movement was at the heart of educational and social change. At a California Campus Compact conference in San Diego, this suppressed history emerged in the charged dynamics between the mostly white administrators and faculty and those people of color who challenged the prevailing definition of community. In southern California, the community is often immigrant or racially diverse. The routinizing of service and the platitudes about community (usually laced with Tocqueville) obscure the roots of service in the civil rights movement, especially for African American and other ethnic groups. White students sent into "the community" (read "poor and of color") have quite a different history than, say, Chicano students who are not "sent" into the community but who seek to bring their concerns into the academy with them. It is the historical difference between John F. Kennedy's call to service and the emerging counterinstitutions of César Chávez and Ella Baker.

Members of early social movements argued for a pedagogy that was transformative, a pedagogy that sought to create awareness and change social relations through activism. As Freire argued (1995, 29), any approach to the community that does not have transformation as a goal is "false charity": "An unjust social order is the permanent fount of this generosity, which is nourished by death, despair, and poverty." This is now referred to as one of several "models" of community learning, the word *model* standing in for the word *ideology*. While I am also unwilling to bully students into political action, I do think it is simplest to present them with the often suppressed history of our curriculum. Our pedagogy should also attempt to engage in cointentional education with the community. Good, contemporary examples exist of taking theater to prisons and poetry to schools, where students learn the subject matter by teaching it.

Reinventing Pedagogy: On Not Using the Master's Tools

In 1979, Audre Lorde succinctly made the connection between method and content in ethnic and women's studies: "What does it mean," she asked, "when the tools of a racist patriarchy are used to examine the fruits of that same patriarchy? It means that only the most narrow perimeters of change are possible and allowable" (111). Reflecting on the 1960s, Alurista (1994) discussed the necessity of changing both the content of courses and the methodology. He argued that the content should provide "an alternative vision, a non-Western view of the world"; but, he noted, all who were discussing Chicano studies were discussing revolutionary studies. Freire provided the model of a dialogic and activist pedagogy. Alurista himself defines radical pedagogy as "leading an individual to discover himself in society." This discovery of community is, of course, the subject of much ethnic literature since the 1970s. Content and pedagogy were, from the beginning, indissoluble.

The original courses in black studies were often created in counterinstitutions, such as the Experimental College in San Francisco. Its "Black Arts and Culture" area was absorbed by the Black Students Union (1967), which offered college credit for student work in the neighborhoods. Students maintained a critical stance toward the university, a stance that now appears in a fairly routinized form—for example, in James Banks's *Multiethnic Education* (1981). Banks offers much good advice, but, again, the activist roots of this pedagogy are elided. Still, the first principle of "multiethnic" pedagogy remains: students should be encouraged to first analyze the school itself as a social and cultural system. Why has the school instituted multicultural or ethnic studies? Is it a numbers game, or is it a true desire to legitimize the ethos of diverse students and achieve democratic access to education? Will the total school environment be changed to reinforce what goes on in isolated classrooms? Banks encourages us to take a holistic and reciprocal view of this new educational process: "The school should be a cultural environment in which acculturation takes place: both teachers and students should assimilate some of the views, perceptions, and ethos of each other as they interact" (107).

Similarly, if a teacher sincerely acknowledges that students already have language and culture (that these are not things teachers give them), the teacher's relationship to the students must change. If we have a diverse classroom, some students will always know more about some texts than teachers do. The teacher identity can no longer be based on an authority of knowledge; rather, knowledge becomes something teacher and students construct together. In a 1994 interview with me, one student succinctly voiced his protest against using traditional authoritarian methods in the multiethnic curriculum: "They want to teach multicultural issues to bring us to them, not to take them to us."

As the teaching practices of many friends and colleagues have taught me, a critical pedagogy in a multiethnic classroom asks students to take different positions in their education: (1) to question course content and hence what knowledge is, (2) to be active learners, and (3) to bridge classroom learning and their communities. They should know that these are essentially the educational demands of past student activists. Since the 1960s have been essentially discredited by the "culture wars" of the 1980s, this information might not impress students. The assignments described later in this chapter might involve them in their own learning in the way that preaching cannot.

Most importantly, teachers should revise their own assumptions about what is worth knowing and about institutional settings in general. There is no fact about American people of color that is not saturated with violence and "politics." This violence is often simply silenced or obscured by spurious ideologies of commonality, such as the melting pot or the tendency to use European immigrants as the model for the experience of people of color. As Ronald Takaki points out (1993, 11), actual commonalities, such as the interethnic collaboration of Japanese and Mexicans in creating unions in 1903, were ruthlessly suppressed.

Interethnic divisions were often manufactured, as in the Virginia miscegenation laws of 1691 that especially targeted white, working-class, or indentured women (Takaki 1993, 67). Thus, any simplistic assimilationist or separatist position must be reexamined, since the very categories and boundaries of culture might be rooted in violence.

Curriculum reform begins with the transformation of the teacher's relationship to knowledge. I admit that I have fallen flat in the classroom while trying to present good material, and that is surely because the institutional setting, the "noise" transmitted by the school environment itself, is far louder than the "content" in any class. As Jules Henry says: "it is not primarily the message that constitutes the most important subject matter to be learned, but the noise! The most significant cultural learnings—primarily the cultural drives—are communicated as noise" (quoted in Lauter and Howe 1970, 233). This is only one more argument for the need to revise pedagogy as well as curriculum and to reevaluate the total school environment. How this might be accomplished is outlined in Alfred Alschuler's *School Discipline* (1980). He adapted Freire's model and discovered that much of the conflict and alienation experienced by students and teachers is generated by the school system itself and not by individual "bad actors." Rules, roles, and regulations literally drowned out what could be said in the classroom.

But the transformation of teachers cannot stop with an awareness of oppression. Teachers' racist assumptions are not truly challenged by teaching the horrors of slavery; they are challenged by learning how to teach the significance of the ring dance and "shouting," for instance, as viable cultural formations. The ability to teach countervalues or alternative perspectives as legitimate sources of knowledge marks a true transformation of knowing within the teacher. Abdul JanMohamed (1990, 9) makes the point that "the very differences that have always been read as symptoms of inadequacy can be reread transformatively as indications and figurations of values radically opposed to those of dominant culture." Equally emphatic is Paula Gunn Allen's assertion (1995, 38) that any valid teaching of ethnic texts must access a culturally specific "critical apparatus that enables a variety of literatures to be explored within their relevant contexts." Like so many teachers and writers, Allen has discovered that our practices are inherently inclusive, based on "actual human society and relationships rather than a textual relationship alone," and are dependent on non-Western "poetic forms that go back hundreds, even thousands, of years."

The issue of countervalues is most important to me because it asks teachers to do what teachers ask students to do, that is, reform their notions of knowledge (and, in my experience, this causes the most resistance among teachers). Even well-intentioned educators are capable of emphasizing what is "deficient" or, on the other side of the coin, what is "universal" in another's sociohistorical experience. The (negatively) unique or the (simplistically) similar are modes of interpretation that maintain the status quo. Similarly, exoticism—reducing other cultures to food, music, dress—presents no challenge to hegemonic ideologies (e.g., "we" have power, and "you" have culture). As Renato Rosaldo points out (1989, 202), there is an inverse power relationship between those who feel they have no culture and those with a high cultural visibility: "as the 'other' becomes more culturally visible, the 'self' becomes correspondingly less so." It is not that those in positions of institutional power lack culture but that they view themselves as normative, universal, and objective. This false omniscience mirrors that of academic claims to "objectivity."

Since overidentification and cultural appropriation have such a long history in America as ways of reinventing the national identity, it is hard to convince teachers and students that they are not sincere forms of flattery. My students fail to see what is wrong with being a Rasta surfer in San Diego (European American males who dreadlock their hair, listen to reggae, and wear the national colors of red, black, and green). They belong to what Rayna Green (1988) calls the "Tribe of Wannabe," usually associated with those who play Indian. From the beginning, pseudotribalism was a way to create the distinctly American as opposed to the European. Even as a form of rebellion, it is a way for the dominant culture to have a dialogue with itself; it depends on genocide and otherwise silencing those whose culture (read "land") produced the countervalues. Green summarizes this complex phenomenon.

> Perhaps relief of guilt is an inherent part of the role, but when taken in connection with other cultural performance epiphenomenon of American life, I have come to think that cultural validation is the role's most important function. For in playing Indian, certainly Anglo-American players are connecting to the America that existed before the European Invasion: they are connecting to the very beginning of the mythical structure called America. (49)

Playing native allows the Anglo-American the murderous fantasy that he/she is the "original inhabitant," as is clearly indicated by bumper stickers that simply read, "Native." The final irony is that actual Native American contributions to American culture (like the agricultural feat of developing the maize plant) are erased from the history books.

Since the conquest of America, the very possibility that indigenous peoples had values has been ruthlessly suppressed. To the extent that we do not humbly try to teach those values (given our linguistic impairment and narrow worldviews), we continue the conquest. We must seriously consider that the Aztecs, for instance, had radically different notions of the earth, salvation, and the role of metaphor and intuition as ways of expressing and obtaining truth (Rodríguez 1994, 7–9). It is no accident that the Chicano literary renaissance was based on an oppositional consciousness forged through neo-indigenous thought.

Like other countervalues, language diversity, both in ethnic texts and in the lives of our students, can create an oppositional consciousness. As Shirley Weber explains (1991, 281): "Language expressed an experience. The experiences of a group are culturally unique; the group will need a different vocabulary to express them." The question of language brings us to the heart of critical pedagogy: will education reproduce (and deracinate) people who adapt to the status quo, or will it create cultural producers who use their differences to humanize and democratize society? Might not the performative quality of Ebonics (African American English) emphasize the importance of what people are as opposed to what they have?

It would contradict my own position to insist that teachers accept my answers to these issues, but teachers must account for the history of those who fought simultaneously for self-determination, cultural autonomy, and universal access to a relevant, liberatory education. Henry Giroux (1993, 118) has provided a definition of this critical pedagogy.

> That is, as a form of engaged practice, critical pedagogy calls into question forms of subordination that create inequities among different groups as they live out their lives. Likewise, it rejects classroom relations that cause difference to be seen as an object of condemnation and oppression, and it refuses to subordinate the purpose of schooling to narrowly defined economic and instru-

mental considerations. This is a notion of critical pedagogy that equates learning with the creation of critical citizens, rather than merely good ones.

Writing Assignments: From Awareness to Taking Action

The following discussion of assignments, both exploratory and (loosely) ethnographic, shows how each kind accomplishes different but complementary ends. Exploratory writing—for instance, in journals—allows students to express insights and feelings incited by readings; this is very important, because many are unwilling to speak their rage, boredom, or joy in class. Such writing also asks students to bridge classroom theory and their own experience, to "problematize" their daily lives. If education is about anything, it is about creating what Freire (1995, 73) called "critical consciousness," based in the "here and now, which constitutes the situation within which they are submerged, from which they emerge, and in which they intervene." Ethnographic assignments, currently understood in composition theory as real-world writing, oral history, or community service writing, have their origin in Freire's notion of students "intervening" in their own communities. Historically, they go back to those undergraduate teachers in pioneering programs, such as the women's studies program at San Diego State University, who gave students credit for boycotting Safeway. Indeed, the United Farm Workers' legendary grape boycott provided an activist training ground for a whole generation of students who learned about social movements with pickets in their hands.

Journals can be particularly effective if we understand that students will go through various stages of awareness. As James Banks testifies, ethnic texts and perspectives are received very differently by diverse, as opposed to mainstream, students. These texts invite microcultural students to (1) recognize their oppression, (2) develop group pride, and (3) voice the needs of the group in a power-sharing model. The texts challenge mainstream students to (1) modify attitudes and stereotypes, (2) understand the psychology of oppression, (3) reconceptualize their notions of society and history, and (4) understand why power sharing is necessary. Both groups are asked to reconceptualize their notions of self. In a class I taught on the Chicano experience, student journals elicited wildly different responses from Anglo and Chicano students. I asked students to write a letter to the writer of the following passage:

> At some point in time every race has been oppressed in some fashion. There are no Swiss or Irish people ranting on about how their people were tortured or misunderstood. . . . I get tired of having to constantly hear about how the Chicanos have been treated unfairly.

Two Chicanos wrote the following entries:

Student 1: "In terms of what history is for, you must keep in mind that we are not only studying the past but also the present. You say that you 'are tired of hearing,' but imagine what it is like to be tired of feeling antagonized, oppressed, treated unfairly, and to feel powerless against it all. Will plugging your ears really resolve the feelings you're having?"

Student 2: "Sensing on racial terms is very new for me and I don't know where this is heading, but I know that this is some sort of cleansing for me."

Using Derald Sue's model for white awareness, it is clear that student 1 is a beginner, in a conformity stage (stage 1), marked by the denial of race as important, yet marked by a rage that is racially motivated. In Sue's five-stage model, the student could potentially move through a dissonance stage (stage 2), where these contradictory feelings are resolved by acknowledging whiteness and institutional racism; a resistance and immersion stage (stage 3), where once racism has been recognized, the student is tempted to respond with paternalism and overidentification (as in the case of the Rasta surfers); an introspection stage (stage 4), where one understands that being white and existing in a racist society cannot be overcome by going native or "doing good"; and, finally, an integrative awareness stage (stage 5), where the student accepts that his/her whiteness must be affirmed and that a nonracist white identity can be created (Sue and Sue 1990, 116).

Since diverse and mainstream students come to class with such radically different emotions, it might relieve them of their guilt and rage to understand that awareness is a process. Once they see the great difference of feeling in class, they will usually be reluctant to speak. Teachers should be prepared for the radically different ways that white students and students of color receive these texts. Obviously, this is the key to classroom dynamics. In a sensitive essay, Sucheng Chan (1989, 275) defines the way she must adjust her presentation of Asian American history to different audiences: "But at the same time, I realized that instead of articulating the experiences of the group—on its behalf, as I had always done—I now had to, instead, translate that experience into terms that non-Asian Americans could comprehend." For students of color, to articulate is to name experiences that are often suppressed; articulation will have a different effect on white students. Journals and anonymous writing can raise and (hopefully) resolve feelings in a way that discussion might not be able to.

In the early weeks of a class, it is crucial to teach the concept of worldview and to encourage students to write about their own. (The term *worldview* might be simply defined as a culture's ideas and assumptions about "the way things are"; it is experienced as what we feel to be "common sense.") Again, because of their unexamined privilege, European American students often feel they are without culture and resent how the ethnic readings empower others and not themselves. An exercise of listing what one takes for granted in the culture, such as the exercise in Peggy McIntosh's "White Privilege and Male Privilege" (1992), might help students access their own cultural norms, especially about race and ethnicity. McIntosh (73–75) writes movingly about the everyday evidences of her own privilege.

> I can do well in a challenging situation without being called a credit to my race. I can choose blemish cover or bandages in "flesh" color and have them more or less match my skin.

Not only should students be encouraged to write down the axioms of their own culture as they explore another, but they should also understand how oppression has changed their lives and not just the lives of the so-called victims. Education, as McIntosh asserts, teaches the pretense that slavery, colonization, genocide have left white lives "as morally neutral, normative, and average, and also ideal": only the oppressed have been dehumanized. Students must understand their own stake in the history and experience they are studying.

We are asking all of our students to become "bifocal," to establish an understanding of another culture without appropriating it or assuming easy identification. Michael Fischer (1986, 199) defines bifocality as "seeing others against a background of ourselves, and ourselves against a background of others." This can probably only occur when there is a constant dialogue that elicits one's own values simultaneously with those of another. What one colleague, Canela Jaramillo, calls "genre subversion" (or any exercise that asks students to try on another form) demonstrates how preferred genres allow certain versions of reality and disallow others, how they reflect the values of a group or the dominant culture, and how messing with them reveals their cultural assumptions. One remarkable student poem led its author, Sarah Long, to confront her own white guilt through a process similar to Derald Sue's. The class was reading "I Am Joaquin," Corky Gonzalez's epic celebration of Chicano nationalism. Trying on the style of this poem and its oppositional nationalism created, I believe, an interior dialogue that nourished an authentic cross-cultural understanding. Clearly, celebrating white nationalism would mean something different; yet Sarah raises serious questions about when any nationalism might become racist or sexist.

Yo soy the daughter of the South
Where my grandfather feeds me banana pudding
While my uncle tells me about lazy niggers

Her quest for an origin myth like Joaquin's forces her to see how such myths involve half-truths. Her envy of those with "culture" and her guilt about historical injustices fuel her search for ethical equilibrium. Her solution, to claim the good and bad in her history, is one we should take to heart.

I am not merely the pale oppressor,
But it is a part of me.
Now it is left to me to find the courage to claim it.

Both Sarah's relationship to history and her identity have changed. By translating course material according to her own experience and worldview, she has probably understood it better than do those who give it back to us in academic legal tender.

Ethnographies in Common Places

As the activists of the 1960s and 1970s insist, community is at the heart of critical pedagogy, and an emphasis on community invites what we might loosely call "ethnographic assignments." Shirley Brice Heath's *Ways with Words* (1983) is the classic study of how such techniques contribute to improved student competence. Heath writes:

> In any case, unless the boundaries between classroom and communities can be broken, and the flow of cultural patterns between them encouraged, the schools will continue to legitimate and reproduce communities of townspeople who control and limit the potential progress of other communities and who themselves remain untouched by other values and ways of life. (309)

This important statement not only validates the students' home culture but demands a reciprocal community exchange. Intercultural education should begin with the school culture itself, the primal scene of so much suffering, as ethnic text after text testifies. Not even privileged students neatly adapt to school culture, and the alienation they feel can help them understand the matrix of the competing and often contradictory norms in which we exist.

The ethnographic projects outlined next both bridge and describe the social and cognitive systems of meanings in the classroom and community. Writing an oral history or family history, for instance, validates both oral and written sources. Students are encouraged to view older people or people of different ethnicities as sources of knowledge. Furthermore, they are now the experts on their material, reversing the usual practice of teachers presenting information to students (Heath 1983, 342).

As students, teachers, and community members construct their projects, they will have to resolve many of the issues of contemporary ethnography. Will the student present himself/herself as an "objective observer"? What opportunities will the "informant(s)" have for self-representation or even coauthorship? How will the student project benefit or be returned to the informant(s)? Then, the student must choose the appropriate form for the material, perhaps deciding that a narrative will best present the ambiguities of actual encounters. James Clifford (1988, 15) summarizes the complexities of the new ethnography.

> It locates the cultural interpretations in many sorts of reciprocal contexts, and it obliges writers to find diverse ways of rendering negotiated realities as multisubjective, power laden, and incongruent. In this view "culture" is always relational, an inscription of communicative processes that exist, historically, between subjects in relations of power.

Four projects that involve ethnographic and/or "real-world" writing are (1) the oral history, (2) community service writing, (3) the proposal for curriculum change, and (4) action projects. Projects using oral histories or interviews can be structured in a variety of ways; they can be collected as important new material, or they can supplement library research. Doing interviews can often be revelatory for students; they no longer merely collate the findings of others but generate their own data and evaluate living experts. San Diego is especially rich in opportunities for crossing the line into other communities. One student, José Lucero, for whom Tijuana "was just a passage point, a blur on the way to America" as he himself crossed as a child, returned to the *ciudad perdida* to tutor adults. His experimental essay/testimonial/oral history interweaves research, a diary of his visits, interviews, and even a piece of student writing by "Noelia": "Well, my life began when I was born, when I remember that a world existed in which I was raised. I am, and belong to a humble but very well-mannered family. I don't know why then I turned out so *bromista*." José's complex written response solves the problems of writing culture, of "rendering negotiated realities as multisubjective, power laden, and incongruent" as outlined by Clifford.

Community service writing is, in some ways, the best and the most problematic activity for ethnic or women's studies. As I have argued in the preceding historical overview, the contradictions exist in the campus "volunteer" or "community" resource centers. These centers often do an excellent job of connecting various students with agencies, but they are not always as articulate about the questions of power, racism, and paternalism that students confront. Service learning is often defended according to a skills-based argument: students who write for an agency, say a Catholic charity newsletter, learn more about editing and audience than do other students. But it is crucial that teachers also ask students such questions as, How do we assess the place of the organization in the community?

Much is also made of how community service writing redistributes authority in the classroom. Students know more about their communities and subjects than teachers do. Teachers must respond in an ad hoc way to student questions about methodology and resources, and I agree that this can only be viewed as a kind of success. But, again, the community of learners in the classroom should not be confused with the broader community. Students may well be the oppressed, but we are sending them into the world not as the oppressed but as workers and investigators who are there to establish a reciprocal relationship with community members. A pedagogy that submerges the relationship between student and community seems to me to pervert the model by Friere that so many invoke.

Just as students and faculty designed the "first" courses in ethnic or women's studies, so students can still be involved in curriculum reform. One student at Stanford wrote a proposal for incorporating Holocaust literature into the freshman course "Europe and the Americas." Her critique of the course demonstrates a sophisticated grasp of its contents.

> At Stanford, I have faced the need to articulate my Jewish identity. . . . How can I explain that, skin color aside, I do not consider myself white? . . . Like Maxine Hong Kingston, I am challenged by the dichotomy between how I view myself and how others view me. Like Sandra Cisneros, I question whether my culture is a subset of the dominant culture or a separate entity. Like Rigoberta Menchu, I have chosen to take pride in my identity and stand as a spokesperson. I may not have found answers, but I have found solace in the idea that I am not alone.

The range of styles and the polyvocality in her proposal is impressive: she includes a personal statement, a more "objective argument" for the inclusion of Elie Weisel in the course, study questions, and a moving interview with her grandfather. This chorus of written voices creates a web of meaning more powerful than any single linguistic register could.

James Banks, in *Multiethnic Education* (1981, 219), describes a final category of assignments as "action projects." Many disciplines are diversifying their curricula, and Banks encourages teachers to go beyond collecting data to the formulation and implementation of courses of action. For example, Banks asks students to conduct a survey to determine what local housing laws exist and whether or not they are enforced. Students develop recommendations from the survey and present them to the appropriate officials. A coalition of students at my present university in San Diego formulated their own "action project" and wrote a proposal directed to the president of the university, expressing the need for a multicultural center. While this writing took place outside the classroom, it was the kind of project that teachers should strive to incorporate into their curriculum; the benefits of writing for an audience, not to the assignment, are obvious. Such a project can be designed so that all students do some writing—something that clearly did not happen with our students. Obviously, it is especially important to empower those students who feel shame about their self-presentation on paper.

Conclusion

I realize that the discussion in this chapter has been wide-ranging, and I hope that it is clear why this must be so. Radical pedagogy, composition theory, and ethnic and women's studies came from a historical moment. My return to people in the movement is not, I hope, a nostalgia trip but a return to history and to the crucial idea of praxis that informed all those movements. These assignments and this pedagogy arise from the idea of community, which is the most important legacy of the 1960s and 1970s. Praxis assumes a dialectic between theory and actual human situations. National standards to the contrary, education happens in a specific place. There will always be a tension between the Kantian "public world" of scholarly exchange and what Kant significantly misnames the merely "private" world of civic life. Who defines what the community is will be and must be contested. Pedagogical innovations like experiential learning must be equally scrutinized; they are often so narrowly defined that their transformative potential is negated (i.e., the power relations within them are mystified). If the root of community is "common," the task of establishing connections where they might be denied will be an ongoing struggle.

The movement in classroom projects from consciousness raising—or what we now call "finding our voice"—to action can be seen in retrospect to have a clear history. Textbooks focus on "finding a voice" as if that were a self-sufficient goal; but we do so to say what? Only a renewed sense of commonality can answer this, and this insight has been the gift of so many women writers and writers of color. Proclaiming the self inevitably begins with the pain experienced as a member of a community; redemption, then, is also communal. José Lucero, a student whose community service writing led him back to the border city of Tijuana, discovered this on his own and expressed this in words more eloquent than mine: "It has not been until recently, partly because of my desire for the feeling of independence, and partly because of my need to reconcile with my culture and people (the two reasons, I believe, go hand in hand), that I've voluntarily gone into the city." Only "local knowledge," as they say, and only a change of curriculum and pedagogy—the integration of theory, praxis, academic culture, and home culture—could produce his level of critical and cultural literacy.

While my students and I live on a real, not a metaphorical, border, there is a true sense in which ethnic studies and critical pedagogy imply a critique of all boundaries, from international checkpoints to professional gatekeepers. As Allen writes (1995, 34), our very discipline requires a "dizzying class-crossing from the fields to the salons, from the factories to the academy, or from galleries and the groves of academe to the neighborhoods and reservations." Perhaps our students best model, just as they did thirty years ago, the compassion and courage necessary to be a border crosser. Few can match the words of Pedro Ríos, a Chicano Literature student who staged his own "illegal" border crossing to "see what it was like."

> I took the first step into the forbidden zone as the rush of the experience began. Without hesitation, I ran through the shadows, followed by my cousin, whose breath I could just make out. I was undocumented for just a night, but for that night, it felt like I had been that way forever.

Works Cited

Allen, Paula Gunn. 1995. Border studies: The intersection of gender and color. In *The ethnic canon,* ed. David Palumbo-Liu. Minneapolis: University of Minnesota Press.

Alschuler, Alfred. 1980. *School discipline: A socially literate solution.* New York: McGraw-Hill.

Alurista. 1994. Interview by author. San Diego, CA, 22 July.

Banks, James. 1981. *Multiethnic education.* Newton: Allyn and Bacon.

Brodkey, Linda. 1996. *Writing permitted in designated areas only.* Minneapolis: University of Minnesota Press.

Chan, Sucheng. 1989. On the ethnic studies requirement. *Amerasia* 15, no. 1:267–80.

Clifford, James. 1988. *The predicament of culture.* Cambridge: Harvard University Press.

Collins, Patricia Hill. 1991. *Black feminist thought.* New York: Routledge.

de la Torre, Adela. 1996. Activism isn't enough any more. *Los Angeles Times,* 12 December, B-9.

Fischer, Michael. 1986. Ethnicity and postmodern arts of memory. In *Writing culture,* ed. James Clifford and George Marcus. Los Angeles: University of California Press.

Freire, Paulo. 1970. *Pedagogy of the oppressed.* New York: Continuum.

———. 1995. *Pedagogy of hope.* New York: Continuum.

Galura, Jeff, Jeffrey Howard, Dave Waterhouse, and Randy Ross. 1995. *Praxis III: Voices in dialogue.* Ann Arbor: OCSL Press.

Giroux, Henry. 1993. Paulo Freire and the politics of post-colonialism. In *Paulo Freire: A critical encounter,* ed. Peter McLaren and Peter Leonard. London: Routledge.

Green, Rayna. 1988. The tribe called Wannabe. *Folklore* 99.

Guerrero, M. Annette Jaimes. 1996. Academic apartheid. In *Mapping multiculturalism,* ed. Avery F. Gordon and Christopher Newfield. Minneapolis: University of Minnesota Press.

Heath, Shirley Brice. 1983. *Ways with words.* Cambridge: Cambridge University Press.

hooks, bell. 1994. *Teaching to transgress.* New York: Routledge.

Hu-DeHart, Evelyn. 1993. The history, development, and future of ethnic studies. *Phi Delta Kappan* 13 (September): 50–54.

JanMohamed, Abdul R. 1990. Introduction: Toward a theory of minority discourses. In *The nature and context of minority discourse,* ed. Abdul R. JanMohamed and David Lloyd. New York: Oxford University Press.

Kirkwood, Carla. 1994. Interview by author. San Diego, CA, 10 August.

Lauter, Paul, and Florence Howe. 1970. *The conspiracy of the young.* New York: World.

López, Ian Haney. 1993. Community ties and law school faculty hiring: The case for professors who don't think white. In *Beyond a dream deferred,* ed. Becky W. Thompson and Sangeeta Tyagi. Minneapolis: University of Minnesota Press.

Lorde, Audre. 1983. *Sister outsider.* Freedom, CA: Crossing.

McIntosh, Peggy. 1992. White privilege and male privilege: A personal account of coming to see correspondences through work in women's studies. In *Race, class, and gender: An anthology,* ed. Margaret L. Anderson and Patricia Hill Collins. Belmont, CA: Wadsworth.

Muñoz, Carlos. 1989. *Youth identity and power.* New York: Verso.

Nower, Leon, and Joyce Nower. 1994. Interview by author. San Diego, CA, 5 August.

Rodríguez, Jeanette. 1994. *Our Lady of Guadalupe.* Austin: University of Texas Press.

Rosaldo, Renato. 1989. *Culture and truth.* Boston: Beacon.

Sue, Derald Wing, and David Sue. 1990. *Counseling the culturally different.* New York: John Wiley and Sons.

Takaki, Ronald. 1993. *A different mirror: A history of multicultural America.* New York: Little, Brown.

Weber, Shirley. 1991. The need to be. In *Intercultural communication,* ed. Larry Samovar and Richard E. Porter. Belmont: Wadsworth.

Part 2

Chapter 5

Exploring Diversity in the Writings of Asian American Students

Franklin Ng
California State University, Fresno
Fresno, CA

In the past few decades, American society has witnessed a wide-ranging debate about the courses and readings that would be desirable in an undergraduate education. Framed against a background of the United States becoming an increasingly diverse society, the debate has often focused on what should constitute the core of a university curriculum. Should the classics of Western civilization, such as the works of William Shakespeare or John Milton, occupy center stage in the education of undergraduate students? Or should there be an attempt to incorporate into the curriculum the classics of other, non-Western civilizations and works by writers of color in the United States?

Described as "culture wars," a contest between a unitary culture and multiculturalism, the struggle has commanded the interest of the public and the press. In many respects, the furor keys in on what constitutes information worth knowing. It is a conflict that has surfaced repeatedly in American history, in the quest for a broad and liberal education. The title of, for example, Charles van Doren's book *A History of Knowledge: Past, Present, and Future* (1992), which conveys a sense of certitude, hardly hints at the Sturm und Drang that has developed over the definition of "worthwhile" knowledge.

The adversaries in the debate over the appropriate canon for the undergraduate curriculum are well known. Individuals frequently identified with the Western canon, although they do not necessarily echo a common refrain, are E. D. Hirsch, Jr. (1987), Alan Bloom (1987), Dinesh D'Souza (1991), Arthur M. Schlesinger, Jr. (1991), and Lynne V. Cheney (1995). Challenging their ideas, in one form or another, are, for example, Becky W. Thompson and Sangeeta Tyagi (1993) and Lawrence Levine (1996). *The Dictionary of Global Culture* (1997), edited by Kwame Anthony Appiah and Henry Louis Gates, Jr., provides an alternative to Hirsch's *Cultural Literacy* and van Doren's *History of Knowledge*. The cover for the book by Appiah and Gates boldly states that the dictionary is "the global citizen's guide to culture, emphasizing the achievement of the non-Western world—what every American needs to know as we enter the next century." Thompson and Tyagi, Levine, and Appiah and Gates favor inclusiveness and a broader, multicultural approach to education.

Seeking to find a middle ground and to inject some calm into the discussion are David A. Hollinger (1995), Todd Gitlin (1995), and Neil Postman (1995). Gerald Graff (1992) points out that the debate about canon, while heated and emotional, can also prove to be enlightening and beneficial for the process of learning and education. This process of exchanging different views about undergraduate education has now continued for nearly ten years (Leatherman 1997). But even if there is a waning of the debate or if some consensus about a prescription for undergraduate education is achieved, it is not unlikely that the discussion will be reignited at some future time. What constitutes valid knowledge is a question that will be examined and reexamined over and over again as changes occur in American society. As Lawrence Levine notes (1993), change and expanding knowledge requires new approaches—and perhaps revisionism—recognizing new complexities and ambiguities.

Asian American Students on Campus

While the subject of the proper approaches and a suitable canon for an undergraduate curriculum is debated, the issue of teaching writing with a student body that is very diverse is immediate and demands attention. Many campuses now claim student bodies with sizable numbers of Chicano/Latino, African American, Asian American, and European American students. Because universities have writing requirements for their general education classes or concern for writing across the curriculum, students are given many writing assignments and exercises. The hope is that the students will develop their prose skills, as well as their ability to think critically. I have taught general education classes for several years, and since many Asian American students have enrolled in my classes, I will describe my experiences with them. These Asian American students reflect the newer constituencies that are populating U.S. universities, bringing with them different perspectives and diverse life experiences. The views they hold do not necessarily mirror those of second- or third-generation students born in the United States.

Asian Americans are a rapidly growing minority population in the United States. Since the Immigration Act of 1965, the number of Asians has increased dramatically and become much more diverse. Before World War II, people were wont to think of Asian Americans as being primarily Chinese and Japanese, but the situation is different today. More of the new Asian immigrants, those that arrived after 1965, are Asian Indians, Koreans, Filipinos, and Thai. At the end of the Vietnam War, Southeast-Asian refugees from Vietnam, Laos, and Cambodia also joined the Asian American population. These refugees included not only Vietnamese, Lao, and Khmer but also ethnic Chinese, Hmong, Iu-Mien, Lahu, Khmu, Anu Chu, and others (Min 1995).

Even the composition of the Chinese American population has changed. Before 1965, the Chinese in the United States were predominantly Cantonese from Guangdong Province in China, Hong Kong, or Macao. Today, the Chinese Americans also encompass people from Taiwan, Singapore, Southeast Asia, and mainland Chinese provinces other than Guangdong. Earlier Cantonese immigrants were less educated, and many entered as laborers. In recent years, many of the immigrants from Hong Kong, Singapore, and Taiwan are highly educated professionals and are sometimes viewed as constituting a brain drain from their sending areas. Different in terms of education, training, and socioeconomic status, large numbers of the new Chinese immigrants have opted to settle outside of the older Chinatown enclaves. They have moved into suburban areas, rather than settling in enclaves in the inner cities (Fong 1994).

Asian immigration to the United States since 1965 has outnumbered the older Asian American population. As a result, Asian Americans today are primarily foreign-born. The only Asian Americans who are mostly American-born are the Japanese Americans. The strength and expansion of the Japanese economy several years after the American occupation led to smaller numbers of Japanese immigrants as compared to those from other Asian countries. As a result, only the Japanese Americans are predominantly American-born, in marked contrast to all the other Asian American groups.

Asian American Students and the Writing Requirement

It is often said that all politics is local. In a similar way, issues about curriculum are ultimately played out in a local context. In this case, the local context is Fresno, California. In the classroom, one can see the consequences of the immigration legislation of 1965 and the Vietnam War in the makeup of the Asian American students. The majority of them are foreign-born. If the students are American-born, they are likely to be Chinese Americans or Japanese Americans. Many of the Southeast Asian American students are of the "1.5 generation." This phrase was introduced by Korean Americans to refer to those who immigrated to the United States at an early age. Consequently, their experiences and outlooks may be analogous to that of the generation born in America. There is also a growing number of second-generation, Southeast Asian Americans, for over twenty years have passed since the end of the Vietnam War, in 1975.

Students enrolled in classes look to their class syllabi to learn about the organization and content of their courses. My syllabi for my courses spell out the class requirements. There are a number of writing assignments, one of which is a term paper of at least two thousand words, or approximately eight pages. Announcement of this requirement on the first day of class, when there is an orientation and summary of the course outline, immediately induces a mood of fear and panic. Some of the Asian American students dread the prospect of what they think is a lengthy paper.

Predictably, there is a volley of questions about the nature of the paper. I explain to them that the paper is really not that lengthy and that its intermediate length allows them the opportunity to learn how to organize their thoughts about a subject and present it in a clear and cohesive way; that to develop their paper, they may draw on library research, oral interviews, and personal experience and reflection; that a brief description of the paper is to be turned in, as this will help to focus on a topic and will also channel their thinking about the resources they will use and the scope of their paper. Information is also provided about the format of the paper, styles of documentation, and the need to have a duplicate copy of the paper on a diskette, on computer, or in photocopy form.

The questions then take another direction: is grammar going to be a consideration in the grading? A vast literature about the content and methodology of composition instruction exists, but my response is that both grammar and content are important. However, during the course of the semester and before the paper is due, I initiate a brief discussion of grammar. I acknowledge that because many of the students are of the first generation, they may converse in an Asian language with their family. I emphasize that many Asian languages are uninflected (unlike English, articles are not required before nouns) and that because nouns can be plural or singular (similar to the English words *sheep* or *fish*), many Asian American students have problems matching an English noun in the singular or plural case with the corresponding pronoun or verb. Another point I emphasize is that in some Asian languages, verbs do not have conjugations as in English; consequently, a number of the Asian American students usually employ in their writing verb tenses that would be considered incorrect in English.

Selection of Paper Topics

Overall, one of the key problems for the students is the selection of a paper topic and its development. When I announce that students may select their own topics, as long as it is relevant to the course, they are often at a loss in choosing a subject for their paper. Inevitably, they ask for suggestions. This is not surprising; they come from varied backgrounds, and they are concentrating on different areas of study at the university. A number are also first-year freshmen at the university, who have not yet selected a major or discipline. In a multicultural classroom, they do not yet hold well-developed ideas about community, religion, race, ethnicity, gender, and class.

Readers may wonder why I allow the students such broad discretion in selecting a paper topic. An old refrain says, "They little know of England who only England know." Some might argue that the students know little and are not being taxed to expand their intellectual horizons. There is extensive literature about composition and the value of ethnography (Clifford and Marcus 1986; Thompson and Tyagi 1996).

But I believe that it is important to hear student voices, drawn from their communities of memory. I also think that the most successful papers are likely to be those that interest their authors. If the papers are intimately related to the students' communities or everyday lives, they will be so much the better. They will validate and legitimate the students' lives as having information that is worth sharing with others. I encourage the selection of topics that appeal to the students. Can their topics be tied to their majors? Do their topics excite them? Are the topics a part of their own personal experience? Can the students interview people? Do they know of some oral histories worth collecting? All of these considerations may lead students toward a subject for their paper; but they are reminded that, however illuminating their accounts may be, communication in the form of writing readable essays is important. Can they impart insights that will not be obscured or misunderstood? This entails careful attention in terms of written expression and organized exposition.

The students often do not realize that writing up their observations and experiences or conducting interviews can yield valuable sources of information (Spradley and McCurdy 1980). But for examples, one could look at the books edited by Eliot Wigginton in his *Foxfire* series (1972); the essays provide fascinating glimpses of folk practices. Or one could cite the example of Bernhard L. Hormann, who collected papers from students and published them in the journal *Social Process in Hawaii.* The papers, which have been republished in an anthology (Hormann 1968), are straightforward essays about facets of life in Hawaii, yet they offer rich and illuminating insights. To encourage my students in these directions, I mention that if they are in health sciences or nursing, they might wish to write about folk medicine and healing practices. Are there food taboos or beliefs about "hot" and "cold" foods for specific situations? Are there birthing customs and ideas about mothers and young infants? I also note that rites of passage are worth exploring in a paper.

Students in different majors may have other options. Those in criminology may wish to focus on gangs. In Fresno and in California in general, there are Asian male or female gangs with different ethnic backgrounds. The reasons for joining, the activities and colors of gangs, and the problems in leaving them might be possible paper topics. Students of business might select subjects pertaining to marketing strategies that telephone and insurance companies aim at Asian Americans. Is advertising weighted toward men or women? *American Demographics, Transpacific, A. Magazine, Yolk, Face,* and other publications have taken notice of the potential of the growing Asian American consumer market.

Students specializing in mass communications, journalism, theater, or music might wish to pursue topics dealing with stereotypes. Or they might investigate examples of Asian American popular culture, in terms of Asian American musicians, actors, news anchors, or performers. How are Hmong movies, videos, or music CDs made in the United States? How and where do the Vietnamese, Khmer, Lao, and Hmong dub American or Chinese movies into their respective languages? How do television stations and cable channels telecast Asian programs from across the Pacific into the United States? What is the important media for a particular group? Why is it that Chinese-language papers in the United States, such as the *World Journal* and the *International Daily News,* display colorful ads, while papers in the English language are usually a dull, monotonous black?

Developing Topics

The Case Example of Food

Many times, the students seek guidance on how to develop a paper topic. I try to provide them with different examples, illustrating the directions they could take and the questions they could raise. Borrowing a phrase from Clifford Geertz (1973, 3), I emphasize the importance of "thick description." I find food to be a good topic to get them thinking. I happen to be very interested in food and culture, and I even collect cookbooks; however, I like to acquire the cookbooks put out by community groups, rather than those distributed by commercial publishers. The first-generation immigrants usually know how to prepare dishes, but the second generation does not. Yearning for the home-cooked dishes that their parents made, they want to collect the recipes. If they purchase the cookbooks printed by commercial publishers, quite often the recipes are for formal occasions—what one might call banquet food—and do not showcase the daily or regionally distinct dishes usually prepared by their parents.

That is why community-based cookbooks are so fascinating. They acknowledge the regional origins of the immigrants and include the dishes prepared by the first-generation immigrants. Knowing that the

American-born generation is unaware of traditional customs, cookbooks may transmit folk wisdom in the form of sayings and taboos. Birthing practices and folk remedies are included along with favorite recipes. The symbolism behind rituals and practices may also be spelled out. So, in a general way, the appearance of cookbooks demarcates the coming-of-age of a sizable second generation. Knowing this significance, I talk to my students and ask them to be on the lookout for Lao, Vietnamese, Cambodian, Filipino, Asian Indian, Korean, Taiwanese, and Hmong cookbooks.

That food and culture are related is a truism. For example, many Southeast Asian refugees came from backgrounds in which they were unaware of refrigeration or of electric and gas appliances. When they came to America, many of them did not know which foods belonged in a refrigerator, a pantry, or a cupboard. Should eggs be refrigerated? How about peanut butter or bread? Which foods should be cooked in a toaster, miniature grill, stove, or microwave oven? I know of butchers who told of Southeast Asian refugees going down to markets in the afternoon, fully expecting meat prices to be discounted; that was the traditional practice with hawkers in their homelands, as there was no refrigeration. Some also tell about Southeast Asians trying to feel meats to be sure that they are fresh instead of being old or refrigerated, as their traditional food values placed a premium on freshly slaughtered meat.

When they first arrived in the United States, many Asians—an example might be the Hmong—preferred to purchase live chickens. After killing the chicken, they defeathered and prepared it, gizzards and all. But in many urban supermarkets, they only see chicken breasts, thighs, and wings. Certainly they will not as easily be able to get the live chicken with its legs, heart, and neck. And if they purchase a whole chicken, it is beheaded and without feathers or blood. Members of the second generation may not know about these practices, or else now they prefer convenience over traditional food ways.

One might think that the Southeast Asian refugees are helpless, since they are unfamiliar with American society. Many of them, however, are quite inventive and resourceful. Throughout California, there are many Cambodian donut shops (Mydans 1995). They usually employ the spelling *donut,* instead of *doughnut,* because it uses fewer letters and therefore the signs are cheaper to buy. In a form of ethnic occupational specialization, Cambodians have become identified with donut shops. One earlier pioneer entered the business and then taught others to enter the business. They work hard for long hours in family businesses instead of being unemployed (Lee 1996).

In Fresno, there are several Cambodian donut shops. Reading their signs, one is startled to see that they also offer hamburgers and Chinese food. At first glance, one would be hesitant to buy Chinese food from a place that sold hamburgers and donuts. At the same time, one would hesitate to buy hamburgers or donuts from a place that sold Chinese food. The food offerings seem odd and incongruous to many observers. But since the Cambodians—in this case, Chinese Cambodians—are unaware of American ideas about food domains or food ways, they have mixed several categories together. Knowing that a business must have a clientele for at least two different mealtimes, they have decided to maximize their business potential. They offer donuts for breakfast, hamburgers for lunch, and Chinese food for dinner. If their businesses fail, onlookers say that they operated with incompatible food items. But if they succeed, it appears that they have invented a new formula, and franchised restaurants based on this model may offer donuts, hamburgers, and Chinese food. They are being creative, like the Chinese vendor who sells egg rolls on a stick at California county fairs or the Japanese in Hawaii who make Spam *musubi,* or rice balls.

The starting of businesses is an intriguing topic. The selling of food and other items through grocery stores is an important avenue for employment. For Southeast Asian refugees, many of whom are not credentialed and do not have fluency in English, starting a business may mean the difference between employment and unemployment. But if they serve their coethnics, especially if they are relatives, some interesting problems can arise. For example, in the case of the Hmong, the community is organized into various clan surnames. Many in the community are related to one another. Since many of them are unemployed, they may turn to a relative who operates a store and ask him to extend credit.

In Laos, the Hmong helped one another in their villages. But in the United States, Hmong- or Lao-operated stores must be able to pay for their inventory via Thailand, China, Taiwan, other countries of Southeast Asia, or the United States. If they extend credit to relatives, the stores may be in danger of defaulting on payments for new supplies. As a result, how the proprietors deal with relatives and coethnics is an interesting and delicate issue.

In the final analysis, foods are a cultural choice. Excluding vegetarians and animal rights activists, people in the United States prefer to eat pork instead of dogs. But from another perspective, pigs are arguably much more intelligent than dogs, so perhaps the latter should be eaten. Whether milk or pork blood should be consumed likewise usually evokes stimulating discussions. But under the guise of Western health and science, there are subtle contests over food choices. In Hawaii, for example, the health department inspectors were successful in getting Chinese roast pork and barbecued pork to be prepared with gas rather than charcoal, to the dismay of food aficionados. They also tried to require that *kalua* pork, a Hawaiian dish for which a whole pig is cooked in an underground oven called an *imu,* should be prepared in regular ovens. They were, however, unsuccessful in banning the sale of pork lungs, brains, blood, kidneys, and spleens. More recently, in 1996, they argued that *musubi* and *obento* (Japanese box lunches) had to be refrigerated.

These struggles are reminiscent of the controversy over Chinese roast duck in California during the tenure of Governor George Deukmejian. California health officials tried to ban the sale of hanging roast ducks unless they were refrigerated, which would detract from their flavor. When a public uproar ensued, with the governor joining the clamor, the health officials retreated. Well-known Western foods—for example, steak tartare and Limburger cheese with bacteria—are accepted, but ethnic foods that are unfamiliar are questioned under the guise of science and public health; in actuality, it is often a contest over food values.

The Case Example of Beauty Pageants

Almost any topic can be worth examining if it is approached with a sense of wonder and curiosity. To take another example, one could draw from popular culture and discuss the Miss Hmong beauty pageants. For several years now, during the Hmong celebration of their New Year in Fresno in late December, after Christmas, there has been a Miss Hmong beauty pageant. Because Fresno boasts the largest Hmong population of any city in the United States, Hmong from all over the world come to participate in this event. From the United States, Hmong from Wisconsin, Minnesota, Oregon, Rhode Island, North Carolina, and other places come to Fresno. Some of the beauty contestants may even come from China and Thailand. In one year, the candidate from China did win the contest.

Watching the Miss Hmong beauty contest is interesting, because one can see a negotiation between Hmong and American criteria for beauty. In one particular year, prominent individuals from outside the Hmong community were invited to participate as judges along with Hmong. A fascinating pattern developed in the judging process. The Hmong judges, who were all men, tended to view the candidates in terms of their being suitable "daughters-in-law"—that is, were they compliant, accommodating, and offering answers that reaffirmed traditional Hmong values, which tended to support patriarchy? In contrast, the non-Hmong judges tended to value independence and assertiveness in the responses from the contestants. In any event, the Miss Hmong beauty pageant can be analyzed on several different levels, one of which is the negotiation of a Hmong-American female identity.

Collecting the Harvest

Once the students are exposed to the wide availability of topics and the ways by which they can develop their papers, they are treated to a rich bonanza of cultural information. The students reveal many insights, going in many directions, some of which those who tout diversity and multiculturalism might not want to hear. For example, one can discern evidence of cultural nationalism. There are revelations of Lao, Hmong, and Cambodian animosity toward the Vietnamese because of conflicts in Southeast Asia. In turn, the Vietnamese and Hmong may harbor a distrust of the Chinese. There are also indications of Korean, Filipino, and Chinese hostility toward Japan for its actions in World War II. The students from these groups are aware of the internment of Japanese Americans in the United States during this period, but some of them share the angry feelings of their parents, grandparents, or community toward Japan and the Japanese in general.

There is also evidence of belief in racial and ethnic hierarchies among the different Asian American groups. Many of the students elect to write papers about interracial dating or marriage. Many of the women indicate a desire to explore beyond the boundaries of their own ethnic group. On occasion, some of them are angry and disappointed by the patriarchal attitudes of the men in their communities. The men, however, usually favor a more comfortable level of dating and marrying within their own ethnic group. They express unease that women from their group may prefer to date or marry others. Both men and women sometimes mention that there is a ranking of different ethnic groups that their parents will accept. With few exceptions, African Americans rank at the bottom.

With respect to their identities, many of my students refer to themselves by their own ethnic group. They separate themselves from others whom they label as Americans. For them, the term *Americans* often refers to European Americans, but it may also refer to African Americans. They consider themselves Chinese, Filipino, Korean, Vietnamese, and so on. Perhaps either a measure of the sense of social distance that they feel or the relative isolation of their families or communities leads them to make these distinctions. For the most part, those who accept those categories are of the immigrant, 1.5-generation, or second-generation background. Japanese Americans who are of the third or fourth generation are more likely to refer to themselves as Americans. Many of my students tend to see the loss of ethnic and cultural identity as acculturation takes place. They do not necessarily see ethnicity as being situational or nonlinear, or as an identity that may be constructed and reconstructed through time.

One can detect feminist attitudes among some of the Asian American women students. Many stress the importance of an education and a career instead of early marriage. Many Hmong female students in particular are already married when they enter the university. Some feel that the need to take care of children and a husband is a handicap to their educational advancement. Some admit that they will not compel their own daughters to get married at an early age as is the usual Hmong practice. One Hmong male student, who stated his age as twenty-five, said that he knew that he should not marry a young Hmong female but that he could find no Hmong female available at his age, as they had all been "taken." As a result, he admitted, he had his eye on a beautiful fourteen-year-old girl.

The students are aware of the differences between Asians in Asia and Asian Americans in the United States. But if their papers are any indication, the prospect for pan–Asian American unity or ethnicity (Espiritu 1992) is low among my students. Once one gets beyond the politicizing by activist organizations, the evolving identities of Asian American students is very much in flux. Filipino Americans think primarily in terms of their own group. The Lao, Hmong, Vietnamese, and Cambodian students have sometimes questioned the use of the terms *Southeast Asian* or *Indochinese.* They prefer to be known by their own individual identities. Although other minority groups on campus, such as African Americans and Chicano/Latinos, have suggested that Southeast Asian American students have more in common with them than with the Chinese and Japanese Americans, no affiliations have occurred. Yet Filipino Americans find African American rap and hip-hop posturing fascinating and have tried to incorporate some of that "attitude" into their behavior.

Asian American students can provide interesting examples of transnationalism and immigrant nationalism. Vietnamese students, for example, have written about their parents' hatred of Hanoi and the communists. At the same time, some in the Vietnamese community have faithfully sent parcels and food to relatives and friends in Vietnam. The Hmong students talk about a number of resistance movements in Thailand and northern Laos that are hoping to topple the communist government of Laos. One major resistance group is the Neo Hom, led by General Vang Pao (Pfaff 1995, 74). Some students indicate that their parents have strong views on this issue and discourage their children from questioning or raising doubts about this matter. Among some of my Khmer students, there was a desire that peace could be brought to Cambodia and that the greatness of the former Khmer empire could be restored. Southeast Asian American students sometimes mention that a desire to return to the homeland is the reason that many of their parents have not moved from a permanent residency status to becoming naturalized U.S. citizens.

The students declare that the firm sense of anticommunism is deeply held among their parents. In their papers, they often remark that because they came as refugees, the Southeast Asians are different from other Asians who came to the United States. However, they—and many members of the media as well—have forgotten that there were also Chinese refugees fleeing from Communist China after World War II. What is startling is that a number of the students are looking forward to business opportunities with communist countries. This includes students who are Vietnamese, Hmong, Lao, and Cambodian, as well as a few Chinese. These students see the Pacific Rim as the future and anticipate opportunities developing in Vietnam, Cambodia, Laos, and China.

Religion also is a common topic among my students. Some, for example, have written about Asian Bible study groups. Filipino students have shared insights about their Catholic faith or their ties to the Iglesia ni Kristo churches. Vietnamese students have touched on their Christian or Buddhist beliefs. One interesting paper discussed the gulf and tension between Vietnamese Catholics and Buddhists. Its author commented how he was having difficulty in persuading a Catholic family to allow their daughter to date a Vietnamese Buddhist. To offer another example, the Lao and Cambodian students talk about their temples and ties to the Theravada branch of Buddhism. Chinese and Japanese students discuss Christianity or Mahayana Buddhism, while my Asian Indian students discuss their Sikh or Hindu beliefs. None of my students has as yet written about Islam and the local mosque.

The subject of conversion to Christianity or resistance to it is a popular theme in many of the papers about religion. This struggle seems to be the most intense among the Hmong. Coming from a preliterate background, with shamanism as their traditional practice, many of the Hmong feel as if they have been hurled into another dimension by coming to America. Familiar with preindustrial farming but not with the technology of the United States, they feel as if they are strangers in a strange land. Sensing inferiority and inadequacy, some first-generation Hmong feel elevated and more integrated into their new host society by conversion to Christianity. Conversion may also result from students' sense of obligation to their Christian sponsors. A generational cleavage has thus developed, with some parents holding onto their shamanistic practices while their children, who are attending schools or universities, have elected to convert to Christianity. Some of the younger Hmong, however, are struggling to find a basis for accommodating shamanism into American society.

A sizable number of my students are majoring in liberal studies in preparation for entrance into programs to obtain their teaching credentials. At one point, some of these students wrote papers criticizing the California Basic Educational Skills Test (CBEST), which they felt discriminated against Southeast Asian American students, who had less fluency with English (Cheng and Ima 1988). Failure to pass the CBEST precludes one from becoming a regular teacher within the state's public schools. At the present time, many of the students support the CBEST, feeling that it is a safeguard for good teaching standards and preparation. Very interesting to me is the fact that some of my students have written papers opposing bilingual education as an albatross around the neck of the younger members of their community. One student in particular felt that it was an insidious form of tracking. Overall, the students did not represent a consensus on this issue, as there were those who took the opposite view.

The Tao of Openness

As one can see, I permit a wide variety of topics to be written about in my classes. By being relatively open, I try to avoid the role of gatekeeper or guardian in limiting the scope of their papers, even if they touch on potentially sensitive or controversial subjects. I allow the students wide latitude to pursue their interests. One might almost say I maintain a Taoist stance of openness and afford students the cultural space to be themselves. As Lao-tzu put it:

> If I keep from meddling with people, they care for themselves,
> If I keep from commanding people, they behave themselves,
> If I keep from preaching at people, they improve themselves,
> If I keep from imposing on people, they become themselves.

It is clear that student interests are often linked to deeply held, emotional beliefs. Because I do not require a particular political or social orientation from my students, the range of opinions and ideas I receive is quite wide. As can be seen, I receive rather unbridled, freewheeling commentaries. The student narratives touch all aspects of the political spectrum. They present discourses that sometimes collide with notions of what is politically correct as advocated by proponents of multiculturalism and diversity. Some of the students unquestionably have a self-inflated sense of importance. They feel their expositions are novel revelations and that they are imparting to me a hidden wisdom that they wish to share.

Depending on the semester, the students turn in their papers either before Thanksgiving vacation or before the spring recess. That way, I have sufficient time to read and grade the papers. I give attention to matters of content and form, usually providing pointers, corrections, observations, and comments. After returning the papers, I then have the opportunity to share some of the students' ideas with others in class. Some come away with a profound respect for their peers, while others are startled by the diverse points of view represented in the class. Students find the ideas expressed by their peers enlightening, thought provoking, disturbing, and stimulating. The discussions that follow help to complement the class presentations and the course readings.

Conclusion

As universities become more diverse in their student populations, educators debate about the type of undergraduate curriculum that would be most desirable. However individuals weigh in on this issue, almost all agree that effective writing is a vital component of the undergraduate curriculum. Hence, one always hears the mantra to implement "writing across the curriculum." In my classes with Asian American students, many of whom have anxiety about writing, I encourage the students to write about topics of personal interest. I try to direct them to focus on autoethnography, ethnography, and other subjects that might engage their attention. I try to get them to value their own voices, their own memories, and their own narratives. They engage in reflexive thinking, questioning sometimes their own assumptions, those of their community, and those of the larger society. In pursuing this kind of interrogation, they learn to be critical thinkers and also to be aware of competing points of view.

By permitting students to write about topics in which they profess interest or command some knowledge, I am privy to a wide range of opinions and ideas. The resulting student discourses and narratives, together with their interesting subtexts, reveal a vast array of perspectives, many of which challenge notions of political correctness. Examples of ethnocentrism, immigrant nationalism, acceptance of racial hierarchies, class bias, indifference to discrimination, preference for assimilation as opposed to multiculturalism, and other trends can be detected. Opposite views can also be observed. At the same time, the student writing is frequently informed by rich insights about community, religion, race, ethnicity, class, and gender. Reading this rich bonanza is not an instance of exploiting the students but an example of acknowledging diversity and respecting the students' values, beliefs, and persons. In any case, as these students develop their skills in writing and critical thinking, they realize some of the most important goals in their own undergraduate education.

Works Cited

Appiah, Kwame Anthony, and Henry Louis Gates, Jr., eds. 1997. *The dictionary of global culture.* New York: Knopf.

Bloom, Allan. 1987. *The closing of the American mind: How higher education has failed democracy and impoverished the souls of today's students.* New York: Simon and Schuster.

Cheney, Lynne V. 1995. *Telling the truth: Why our culture and our country have stopped making sense—and what we can do about it.* New York: Simon and Schuster.

Cheng, Li-Rong Lilly, and Kenji Ima. 1988. The California basic educational skills test (CBEST) and Indochinese teacher interns: A case of a cultural barrier to foreign-born Asian professionals? In *Reflections on shattered windows: Promises and prospects for Asian American studies,* ed. Gary Y. Okihiro, Shirley Hune, Arthur A. Hansen, and John M. Liu, 67–79. Pullman: Washington State University Press.

Clifford, James, and George E. Marcus, eds. 1986. *Writing culture: The poetics and politics of ethnography.* Berkeley: University of California Press.

D'Souza, Dinesh. 1991. *Illiberal education: The politics of race and sex on campus.* New York: New Press.

Espiritu, Yen Le. 1992. *Asian American panethnicity: Bridging institutions and identities.* Philadelphia: Temple University Press.

Fong, Timothy. 1994. *The first suburban Chinatown: The remaking of Monterey Park, California.* Philadelphia: Temple University Press.

Geertz, Clifford. 1973. *The interpretation of cultures.* New York: Basic.

Gitlin, Todd. 1995. *The twilight of common dreams: Why America is wracked by culture wars.* New York: Metropolitan.

Graff, Gerald. 1992. *Beyond the culture wars: How teaching the conflicts can revitalize American education.* New York: Norton.

Hirsch, E. D., Jr. 1987. *Cultural literacy: What every American needs to know.* Boston: Houghton Mifflin.

Hollinger, David A. 1995. *Postethnic America.* New York: Basic.

Hormann, Bernhard L., ed. 1968. *Community forces in Hawaii: A book of readings.* Honolulu: University of Hawaii.

Leatherman, Courtney. 1997. Ten years after Bloom's Jeremiad, scholars weigh its significance. *Chronicle of Higher Education,* 17 January, A14–15.

Lee, Gen Leigh. 1996. Chinese-Cambodian donut makers in Orange County: Case studies of family labor and socioeconomic adaptations. In *Reframing the immigration debate,* ed. Bill Ong Hing and Ronald Lee, 205–19. Los Angeles: LEAP Asian Pacific American Public Policy Institute and UCLA Asian American Studies Center.

Levine, Lawrence. 1996. *The opening of the American mind: Canons, culture, and history.* Boston: Beacon.

———. 1993. *The unpredictable past: Explorations in American cultural history.* New York: Oxford University Press.

Min, Pyong Gap, ed. 1995. *Asian Americans: Contemporary trends and issues.* Thousand Oaks, CA: Sage.

Mydans, Seth. 1995. From Cambodia to doughnut shops. *New York Times,* 26 May, A8.

Pfaff, Timothy. 1995. *Hmong in America: Journey from a secret war.* Eau Claire, WI: Chippewa Valley Museum Press.

Postman, Neil. 1995. *The end of education: Redefining the value of school.* New York: Knopf.

Schlesinger, Arthur M., Jr. 1991. *The disuniting of America.* New York: Norton.

Spradley, James P., and David W. McCurdy. 1980. *Participant observation.* New York: Holt, Rinehart, and Winston.

Thompson, Becky W., and Sangeeta Tyagi, eds. 1993. *Beyond a dream deferred: Multicultural education and the politics of excellence.* Minneapolis: University of Minnesota Press.

———. 1996. *Names we call home: Autobiography on racial identity.* New York: Routledge.

van Doren, Charles. 1992. *A history of knowledge: Past, present, and future.* New York: Ballantine.

Wigginton, Eliot. 1972. *The foxfire book.* Garden City, NY: Doubleday.

Chapter 6

Designing Writing Assignments for Exploring Diversity

Terri A. Hasseler
Bryant College
Smithfield, RI

John C. Bean
Seattle University
Seattle, WA

Our premise in this chapter is that writing assignments give teachers a powerful tool for infusing the study of multiculturalism and diversity into courses across the curriculum. Through well-designed assignments, teachers can engage students in multicultural research, introduce them to diverse ways of understanding, and encourage examination of issues of "difference" in their own lives. Within this chapter, we assume a broad definition of *diversity,* ranging from the study of non-U.S. or U.S. minority cultures to the study of ethnicity, class, gender, and sexual orientation.

Using actual assignments from classrooms across the disciplines, we discuss how writing assignments can be designed to help students deepen their thinking about diversity. However, designing assignments about diversity poses a significant problem for instructors: whether to design traditional academic assignments requiring thesis-based analysis and argument or more narrative assignments inviting students to disclose and examine personal events in their own lives. In the first section that follows, we develop this problem in detail, laying out the contending values of thesis-based argument versus personal forms. In the second section, we examine the advantages and potential pitfalls of traditional academic forms; in the third section, we do likewise for personal, inner-directed forms. Finally, in an extensive appendix, we give examples of writing assignments that vary across the spectrum, from the traditionally academic to the highly personal.

The Problem of What to Assign: Academic Argument versus Personal Narrative

Writing teachers frequently distinguish between outer-directed academic argument and inner-directed personal writing. Academic argument, which includes both analytic and persuasive prose, is thesis-based: the writer must define a problem, develop a thesis in response to the problem, use reasons and evidence to support the thesis, attend to opposing or alternative views, create orderly paragraphs exhibiting unity and coherence, and employ other features of logical, well-reasoned prose. Traditionally, term papers or research papers are expected to be thesis-driven arguments, as are various kinds of shorter academic papers requiring persuasion or analysis. Here is a typical multicultural assignment calling for thesis-based argument.

> In class, we have read a variety of articles expressing different points of view on the English Only movement. Write a two- to three-page argument—suitable for publication as a guest piece in the op-ed section of a newspaper—in which you take a stand on this issue, supporting or opposing a constitutional amendment making English the official language of the United States. Support your position with reasons and evidence.

This is only one of many ways to design a writing assignment on the politics of language. Another approach is to focus on what James Britton (Britton et al. 1975) has called "expressive" prose—that is, on personal reflections/narratives or other self-disclosive writing that foregrounds the writer's life and personhood. Expressive assignments—sometimes fulfilled in informal, exploratory modes, such as journal entries or thought letters—ask students to share autobiographical stories, to relate course issues to their own lives, or to write reflectively about the way they see or experience the world. Consider how the previous assignment might be revised from this expressivist perspective.

> In class, we have read a variety of articles expressing different points of view on the English Only movement. Write a paper in which you connect this conversation to your own life. In the introduction of your paper, articulate the position you currently hold on this issue. (You may have a strong view one way or the other on

this issue, but it is also OK to be undecided or confused.) Then, in the body of your paper, explore the life experiences that have led you to your current view. In a personal reflective essay, analyze what personal values and beliefs underlie your position on this issue, and explore how your personal history and experiences have led you to those values.

Of course, these two kinds of assignment—the traditional academic argument and the expressive narrative—are not teachers' only choices. Many teachers assign both personal narrative and academic argument in their courses or create assignments that combine personal experience and argument. But these two poles, when examined in the context of cultural diversity, can yield insight into important issues of assignment design. Both kinds of assignment can open students to multicultural issues, but both have potential pitfalls, which need to be examined. In the following two sections, we examine each assignment type in detail.

Academic Argument: Strengths and Problems

Academic argument has the advantage of being the writing most frequently encountered and traditionally valued in academic and professional life. Argumentative assignments place a premium on critical thinking, reasoned analysis, and careful use of evidence. Because academic argument often requires students to use sources critically and to attend to alternative views, it can help students evaluate and respond to other voices and embrace complexity and ambiguity.

However, teachers who design argumentative assignments can anticipate several problems, many of which can be explained by research in cognitive development. As a number of researchers and theorists have shown—using insights from the stage theories of Perry (1970) or Belenky et al. (1986); from Piaget (Flavell 1963); or from novice/expert theory (Voss 1989)—college writers have difficulty positioning themselves in a controversy, listening to and accommodating opposing views, letting go of cherished beliefs and preconceptions, and opening themselves to growth and change (see, e.g., Hays 1983; Nilson 1997).

It follows, then, that giving students argumentative assignments on multicultural issues will not automatically generate the kind of thinking that the instructor desires. One problem is that many students will write arguments that stridently set out to "prove" their own stereotypes. Because most multicultural issues involve conflicts of values as well as data that are ambiguous and inconclusive, and because inexperienced writers often shut out arguments that contradict their own views, many students neither seriously imagine other points of view nor address the complexities and contradictions of their own stance. To the teacher's disappointment, students submit reductive arguments that assert, often without development or adequate use of evidence, the cherished beliefs with which they began. A related problem is the obverse phenomenon of complete cultural relativism, in which students will accept any view or practice as "OK" for a given culture. Argument becomes a kind of game in which a person can argue any side of any issue. Cultural relativism thus protects students from becoming engaged with contradiction and uncertainty. These two views of argument—as a win/lose battle or a pointless game—can reduce classroom discussions of multicultural issues to clichéd shouting matches or to sterile rehearsals of off-the-shelf pro/con views by students who see nothing at stake.

Fortunately, many of these problems can be overcome by including exploratory writing exercises that precede the formal paper or by altering the assignment itself. The instructor's goal in doing so is to promote open-minded exploration, including the kind of empathic listening to alternative views advocated by psychotherapist Carl Rogers (1961). To encourage such listening, Catherine Lamb (1991) reorients argumentation away from adversarial debate toward negotiation and mediation. She says that writers should use argument "as a means, not an end," adding, "[t]he end—a resolution of conflict that is fair to both sides—is possible even in the apparent one-sidedness of written communication" (11). Instead of teaching students to take a single, hard-nosed position on an issue, Lamb recommends that students "brainstorm a number of possible solutions, evaluating them using criteria both sides can accept" (19), thereby lessening the "distance between writer and audience" (18).

One approach teachers can take is to supplement argumentative assignments with behind-the-scenes exploratory tasks, such as journal entries, thought letters, or in-class "free writes" that cause students to confront the complexity of an issue. (For an array of ways to design exploratory writing tasks, see Bean 1996.) For example, one task might ask each student to interview someone who disagrees with his or her position, to listen carefully to that person's position, and to write reflectively about the experience. Another approach is to vary the assignment itself so that it fosters exploration rather than certainty. Here is an example.

> In class today, we introduced the issue of whether the United States should pass a constitutional amendment making English the country's official language. Your next reading assignment will be a series of articles on this issue. At this time, what is your own initial view on this issue? Explore your view in a five-minute "free write." Then, as you read the articles, identify one that most serves to unsettle your present view or to change your mind. Once you have identified this article, write a three-part paper in which you
>
> 1. describe your initial position on the issue;
> 2. summarize the article that most caused you to question your original position;
> 3. analyze why and how this article caused you to begin to doubt your original position (what reasons and evidence did the author use? why did this argument sway you?).

This assignment, while still requiring analysis and reflection, rewards open-mindedness rather than a hardened position.

Still another strategy for promoting exploration is to help students read as "insiders" rather than "outsiders." These terms, used by Ann Penrose and Cheryl Geisler (1994), describe students' difficulty in claiming authority in their own texts. Penrose and Geisler explain that experienced readers and writers are insiders, who know that "texts and knowledge claims are authored and negotiable," whereas inexperienced writers, or outsiders, approach writing in a "traditional information-transfer model in which texts are definitive and unassailable" (507). According to Penrose and Geisler, outsiders are "uncomfortable with controversy" (511). As a result, when they write, outsiders use evidence in limited ways, trying to find examples to "prove" every point, while neglecting counterexamples. Penrose and Geisler point out that when outsiders encounter conflicting opinions, they tend to avoid complexity through one of two strategies: either they "report" (511) both sides, asking the reader to choose, or they "align [themselves] with one of the positions already available" (512), by arbitrarily picking a side rather than "inserting" (513) the self into the debate.

One way to help students think like insiders is to ask them to reconstruct the thinking processes of each author they encounter in a course. Each time they are assigned a new course reading, they need to ask: What was the problem or issue that inspired this writer to write? What values or beliefs drive this writer's thinking? What evidence or points of view does this writer tend to suppress and why? Who does this writer like and dislike? What is this writer afraid of? The teacher's goal here is to help students understand that views are authored—not unquestioned truths—and that, in Penrose and Geisler's terms, one's "personal knowledge has value" (517).

So far, we have stressed the importance of argument as dialogic exploration rather than as win/lose debate. But the valuing of negotiation and mediation can lead teachers to still another problem when designing an argumentative assignment. Often, issues raised in courses on cultural diversity do not lend themselves easily to the open-minded, mediation model embraced by Lamb and others. For instance, how should an instructor handle a history student who wants to write a paper disproving the reality of the Holocaust or a gay-basher who advocates strict enforcement of existing sodomy laws? Should the instructor accept a mediation and negotiation stance for the sake of "academic freedom," or should the instructor assert his or her own beliefs and values as "true"? There are times, obviously, when teachers need to model for students their own convictions on an issue, times when open-mindedness must yield to a deeply felt conviction that certain positions are simply wrong and that one's integrity is compromised through negotiation.

We do not pretend to know when open-mindedness should yield to conviction in any given situation, but we believe that this problem needs to be addressed. Just as students are bothered by the complexity of open-mindedness, they are bothered by the angry passion of conviction. Jamaica Kincaid's *A Small Place* (1988) is a stunning example of a writer using anger and argument to present the horrors of colonialism and neocolonialism in her homeland of Antigua. Students want to dismiss Kincaid's text because she is "too angry" and because she is specifically angry at the person reading the text, whom she refers to as "you."

Students do not want to be held responsible for her anger and, strikingly, get angry at her in turn, for not just "getting over" her past. Students are uncertain of how to negotiate their own anger and certainly the anger of others. They are puzzled at how anger can be academically "wrong" in, say, shouting matches on trashy talk shows but academically "OK" in Kincaid's case. A too quick rejection of anger will teach students to dismiss rather than understand the role of anger in helping them identify their values and will provide them a ground from which to argue.

The use of argumentative assignments thus raises the dilemma of how to reconcile the competing values of dialogic truth seeking, on the one hand, and dead-certain anger, on the other. None of us can negotiate this dilemma perfectly, but we can help students begin to see a resolution by helping them realize that "truth" is seldom a single, empirically validated answer. More often, it is an answer in context, a personal or social construct rooted in the writer's own values—values that need to be acknowledged, examined, and articulated. Truth seeking is partly a search for empirical data and partly a clarification of one's values—a clarification that often begins with the acknowledgment of anger and with a systematic examination of whether that anger is justified in light of others' views.

A final problem with argumentative assignments is the understanding that the argumentative mode of writing is, itself, a culturally derived form. Some feminist composition theorists have claimed that arguing a thesis privileges a combative, masculine mode of thinking that cuts and divides rather than weaves together (Meisenhelder 1985; Lamb 1991; Bridwell-Bowles 1992). Similarly, the rhetorical patterns of organization and development valued in the Western academy seem at odds with those of other cultures. For example, in her valuable study of cultural differences in writing, Helen Fox (1994, xxi) argues,

> the dominant communication style and world view of the U.S. university, variously known as "academic argument," "analytical writing," "critical thinking," or just plain "good writing," is based on assumptions and habits of mind that are derived from Western—or more specifically U.S.—culture, and . . . this way of thinking and communicating is considered the most sophisticated, intelligent, and efficient by only a tiny fraction of the world's peoples.

In requiring traditional academic argument, instructors may be promoting a particularly Western way of looking at the world. The popularity of more personal and narrative forms, to which we will turn next, results at least partially from this critique of traditional academic discourse.

Personal Narrative: Strengths and Problems

A focus on cultural diversity has caused many instructors to rethink the writing tasks that they have traditionally assigned and rewarded. In this revaluation, inner-directed, autobiographical writing is often posed against thesis-governed, argumentative forms. Personal writing, characterized by a narrative structure that emphasizes the musing voice of the writer while permitting digression, backtracking, and the layering of perspectives, frees the writer from the implied certainty and clarity of thesis-based argument. Many teachers value inner-directed writing because it permits students to think in complex exploratory ways. The constraints of traditional argument cause Bridwell-Bowles (1992) to raise philosophical objections to the whole enterprise of the "standard academic essay." Acknowledging that she had to write "in conventional language, in traditional rhetorical patterns, using accepted research methodologies" (366) to get published and achieve tenure, Bridwell-Bowles now seeks to write in "alternative" or "experimental" forms, which give her

> a more personal voice, an expanded use of metaphor, a less rigid methodological framework, and writing process that allow me to combine hypothesizing with reporting data, to use patterns of writing that allow for multiple truths, what Dale Spender has called a "multidimensional reality," rather than a single thesis, and so on. (350)

Following this bent, many teachers assign inner-directed writing for philosophical as well as pedagogical reasons. According to Linda Peterson (1991), inner-directed writing values "intimacy and richness of detail, highly individual voices and views of experiences, challenges to the status quo, critical stances vis-à-vis the dominant culture or ruling class or patriarchy" (180). Pedagogically, she continues, inner-directed writing serves the important roles of "convincing [students] they have something to say" and "giving them authority over the content of their essays" (179).

Nevertheless, inner-directed assignments raise their own issues and concerns. One problem is that students (and parents) may object to inner-directed assignments as an invasion of student or family privacy. Many political conservatives, in fact, specifically view inner-directed assignments as leftist brainwashing techniques for promoting political correctness. In materials prepared by the Maryland Coalition of Concerned Parents on Privacy Rights in Public Schools, conservative parents objected to "autobiography assignments, log books, diaries, and personal journals," as well as to "contrived incidents for self-revelation," such as "sensitivity training" or other "strategies designed for self-disclosure" (Brown 1994, 63).

Even when students raise no political objections to self-disclosive writing, they are still apt to feel uncomfortable when writing personally about divisive issues. Susan Swartzlander, Diana Pace, and Virginia Lee Stamler, in "The Ethics of Requiring Students to Write about Their Personal Lives" (1993), explore students' difficulty in determining what is appropriate to reveal to whom, as well as the danger that many students, especially women and students of color, may feel at expressing intimate details of their lives to teachers who either may treat their texts in casual ways or are members of the dominant sex or ethnicity. They show how inner-directed assignments tend to demand a therapeutic relationship between student and teacher, in which students have to confront their own issues of gender, ethnicity, or sexuality through writing for the approbation or disapprobation of their teacher/counselor. David Schoem (1991) also emphasizes the risks of self-disclosure. Speaking of his collection of student autobiographical narratives written for his sociology courses, Schoem writes:

> The young authors in this volume take a risk by publishing their stories. Will readers honor the trust that is bestowed by the authors by their open sharing of personal and group "secrets"? Or will readers intentionally misinterpret or abuse such honesty or merely incorporate these stories into the pool of stereotypical misinformation that we all carry with us? (5)

To manage these dangers, Swartzlander, Pace, and Stamler (1993) advise that when teachers use personal and autobiographical writing assignments, they should prepare students early in the semester by explaining that they will be required to use personal forms of writing. Similarly, students will be more likely to trust the experience of personal writing when they learn that the classroom is not the confessional. According to David Bleich (1995, 48), students must learn to make estimations "about the appropriateness and helpfulness to others as well as oneself [of certain personal disclosures]." Teachers can build trust by encouraging students to disclose personal experiences only to the extent that they are relevant to the course discussion and material.

Using personal writing thus requires a safe classroom atmosphere in which students trust others (and the teacher) to accept and value what the student discloses. But this atmosphere of trust can itself be problematic, for it complicates the critiquing of students' ideas and values. Paradoxically, personal and autobiographical forms of writing can constrain classroom discussions, because teachers or classmates often feel that questioning someone's experience is inappropriate. Jerry Mirskin (1995) has noted that when peers critique a classmate's personal essays, they often ask the writer for "more detail" about his or her experience, rather than challenging the writer's interpretation of the experience. By avoiding a questioning or contrary reading, peer critics "save" the feelings of the writer by going out of their way to adopt the writer's value system. Thus, the writer's experience is taken as an unassailable truth; the fact that these events happened is enough. Who would want to dispute whether someone's personal essay is a form of "truth" for that person? This process of avoiding criticism or criticizing corresponds to a strong desire to diminish any form of conflict. Therefore, the amount of trust required for autobiographical writing to work in a classroom might unintentionally subvert a thorough analysis of the subjects addressed, which can be dangerous when those issues are sexism and racism. Teachers who assign inner-directed writing need to develop an atmosphere of trust in which the willingness to affirm the validity of individual experience is balanced against the courage to critique those experiences.

Finally, some of the philosophical or cultural justifications for inner-directed assignments are controversial among teachers. One controversial justification, often asserted by proponents, is that an expressivist assignment can liberate the thinking of women and people of color, who are more attuned to narrative forms that free them from the Western, male, combative constraints of thesis-governed argument.

This proposition, however, implies an essentialist view of gender or ethnicity and reinforces stereotypes of women and "non-Westerners" as nonanalytical thinkers. Moreover, by failing to teach students how to write in a standard academic form, teachers who assign inner-directed writing may subtly reinforce normative, Western, masculine ways of knowing, by keeping their students from gaining the skills needed to enter powerful positions in society.

Conclusion

The preceding analysis of academic argument and personal narrative is intended to help teachers design a sequence of effective writing assignments suited to their own course goals. We believe that both kinds of assignment are valuable, especially if teachers anticipate in advance the problems that may arise. When designing argumentative assignments, instructors should try to push students beyond an us/them dichotomy, which privileges defeating the opponent over dialogic exploration of contradictions and complications. Although students can be urged to support their own convictions rigorously through reasons and evidence, they should demonstrate charitable understanding of differing perspectives. In personal forms of writing, we encourage faculty to design assignments that both respect students' privacy and promote the questioning and critiquing of each others' thoughts and conclusions. Instructors should aim at affirming students' experiences through personal writing; at the same time, however, they should help students develop the courage to critique each other. This relationship is, of course, built on mutual trust, which often takes much time to develop.

We also encourage teachers to find ways to use a variety of assignment types, either by using journal writing or other exploratory writing activities to precede a formal assignment, or by integrating a series of assignments that alternate between personal and academic forms. Our selection of "positioning" pieces in the following appendix is a good example of sequencing. Students can write short exploratory pieces, such as the examples on white and male privilege (example 7) and identity markers (example 8). These pieces can till the soil for a longer academic argument, such as the analysis of the social construction of identity in popular media (example 9). As a general rule, several short, sequenced assignments generate more learning and engagement than does one long assignment. Moreover, the different types of assignments demand different intellectual approaches from students.

Finally, we suggest that instructors should expect to revise their assignments after an initial trial. Assignments that seem effective on paper might not work in the classroom—a problem that teachers should accept as a stimulus for reflection and redesign rather than a cause for dismay. The primary question to ask, we argue, is whether the assignment promoted the kind of thinking and learning that the instructor desired. This question yields better criteria than asking whether the students liked the assignment. Sometimes, assignments are successful because students do *not* like them. Assignments about diversity can be discomforting for students; however, that discomfort can stimulate significant growth in critical thinking and understanding. It is difficult to find a balance between trust and discomfort, but if trust has been developed first, students are more likely to analyze and question why an issue makes them uncomfortable.

APPENDIX: A SAMPLER OF WRITING ASSIGNMENTS ON MULTICULTURALISM AND DIVERSITY

We have arranged the following assignment examples on a continuum from academic argument and analysis to inner-directed and personal forms. These assignments are intended as idea starters only—examples to stimulate the imagination and creativity of individual instructors—rather than as finished models to be transported verbatim from one course to another. We encourage teachers to take from them what works and to modify them at will. The approach an instructor chooses depends, of course, on his or her own course goals, values, and philosophy of teaching. It is important to design assignments that help students achieve the kinds of understanding of diversity and ways of thinking about it that the instructor values.

ASSIGNMENTS FOCUSING ON THESIS-BASED ANALYSIS AND ARGUMENT

We begin at the traditionally academic pole of the spectrum with writing assignments requiring thesis-based analysis and argument.

Advocacy Pieces on Policy Issues

Perhaps the most common argumentative assignments ask students to advocate a position on a public policy issue. We illustrate three possibilities: a "take a stand" assignment (example 1), a behind-the-scenes exploratory narrative (example 2), and a role-playing assignment (example 3).

Example 1

> Choose a public policy issue related to one of the topics of diversity we have discussed in class. Write a three- to five-page argument—suitable for publication as a guest piece in the op-ed section of a newspaper—in which you take a stand on your chosen issue, supporting your position with reasons and evidence. Within your argument, summarize and respond to alternative or opposing views.

An exploratory narrative (e.g., example 2) focuses on truth seeking rather than persuasion and is a good choice if the instructor wants students to wrestle with the complexity of an issue. It calls for a thesis-seeking essay, rather than a thesis-supporting one (see Zeiger 1985; Spellmeyer 1989; Bean 1996; Ramage and Bean 2000).

Example 2

> Our university is currently embroiled in a debate about hate speech. For this paper, write a first-person, chronologically organized account of your thinking process as you explore possible solutions to the problem of hate speech on this campus. Begin by describing your current feelings on the issue. Then, as you contemplate the issue and do research, narrate the evolving process of your thinking. Your exploratory essay should include both external details (what you read, who you talked to) and internal mental details (what you were thinking about, how your ideas were evolving). For this essay, it does not matter whether you reach a final position or solve the problem; your reader is interested in your process, not your final product. In addition to library research, you should include interviews with persons who have strong feelings on various sides of this issue. Your final paper should be eight to twelve pages long.

(For a detailed discussion of exploratory assignments, see Ramage and Bean 2000, 160–92.)

Another way to focus on truth seeking is to ask students to role-play being a policy analyst for a hypothetical legislator. The following assignment, developed by John Bean, effectively deepens students' understanding of the problems of the mentally ill homeless.

Example 3

> You are a newly hired research assistant to Senator Sarah Goodperson. One day you receive from her the following memo:
>
> > [Your name]: I'm being lobbied every which way but loose on the homeless issue, and frankly I'm confused about it. As part of what I need, I would like you to examine the problem of the mentally ill homeless in light of the attached article by Charles Krauthammer from *The New Republic,* which is being avidly supported by a group of psychiatrists and big-city mayors. It advocates reopening state psychiatric hospitals and institutionalizing the homeless mentally ill involuntarily, if necessary. Read what the current literature is saying about the mentally ill homeless and get back to me with your analysis and advice. Should I support Krauthammer's proposal? Are there alternative approaches? Based on your first pass through the literature, which approach do you most recommend and why?

The role-playing aspect of this assignment encourages students to step outside their own preconceptions and see an issue in a richer, more complex context.

Analysis Assignments Requiring Ethnographic Research

Another way to create academic assignments on diversity asks students to do their own ethnographic research. Here is a typical example, developed by Jane Peterson of Seattle University's School of Nursing for a course entitled "The Changing Family."

Example 4

> The purpose of this written paper is to analyze a family from a culture that differs from yours and to understand the implications of a crisis on the family from that family's point of view. The question you are to answer is: What is the effect of ________________ (e.g., sudden infant death, chronic renal failure, monetary crisis, change in job status) on an ____________ (e.g., Indonesian, Italian) family?

1. Identify a key informant from a culture different from your own who is willing to discuss his/her family.
2. Prepare for the interview by reading about the culture and obtaining informed consent.
3. Interview your key informant. If possible, "hang out" with your informant and/or accompany him/her to daily events (e.g., a meal, church) and/or special events (e.g., a birthday, a funeral, a wedding).
4. Keep notes on your interactions with people in the family.
5. Write up your report on how this person/family understands the implications of a crisis and reacts to it.

Peterson's goal is to encourage students to understand the different ways that particular families within different communities respond to crisis situations.

Analysis Assignments Examining Popular Culture

An approach that often engages students asks them to investigate issues of diversity in current films, television programs, print or television advertisements, and so forth. John Bean has developed assignments on advertising that focus on gender, class, or ethnic difference. Here is one example.

Example 5

> Choose two different magazine or television advertisements that sell the same kind of product but appeal to different audiences (e.g., a car ad aimed at men and one aimed at women; a clothing ad from *The New Yorker* and one from *Rolling Stone* or *Ebony*). Describe each ad in sufficient detail so that an audience without access to the ads themselves can easily visualize them. Analyze each ad and explain how each appeals to its target audience. What values are being appealed to in each ad? How is each ad constructed to appeal to those values? Besides analyzing how each ad makes its appeals, you may also wish to evaluate or criticize each ad, commenting on how each both reflects and tries to shape cultural stereotypes.

An assignment like this allows for lively class discussions in which students learn how to "read" media images. Discussion can reveal how advertisers develop psychological and motivational strategies based on the target audience's values and fears, which differ according to ethnicity, gender, educational level, socioeconomic class, and age. Students learn how every feature of an expensive ad, down to the tiniest detail, is the result of conscious choice. To deepen discussion, Bean describes the research of sociologist and semiotician Erving Goffman (1979), who has argued that the way women are pictured in ads (e.g., as decorative rather than instrumental) removes them from serious power. Students see that even when ads try to portray a powerful and independent woman, they often reveal cultural "signs" of subordination.

A variation on this assignment, used by Terri Hasseler, asks teams of students to design a magazine ad marketing an established product for a new target audience (e.g., an ad for personal computers that is to appear in *Mademoiselle*). After designing their ad, the teams must then prepare a proposal argument, written to a hypothetical marketing executive, presenting their design and arguing why they think it will be effective for the target audience. When using this assignment, Hasseler asks students to examine the proportion of ads to articles in various popular magazines, the relationship between the types of ad and the subject matter of articles, and the categories of different kinds of appeal—to sex, to wealth, to social status, and so forth. A strength of this assignment is the high level of student interest it generates. Furthermore, by role-playing as advertisers, students often experience the ethical dilemmas of consumerism—the desire to reform abhorrent images of women, for example, while recognizing that these images sell products.

PERSONAL, INNER-DIRECTED ASSIGNMENTS

We switch now to assignments at the other end of the spectrum, assignments asking students to explore multiculturalism and diversity through the lens of their own lives.

"First Time" or "Awakening" Narratives

A common assignment using personal experience asks students to narrate an event in their lives that awakened them to the existence of racism, classism, homophobia, or other forms of prejudice or that caused them to experience—as either a beneficiary or a victim—the phenomenon of "being different." Here is a typical example.

Example 6

> Choose a moment in your life when you became acutely aware of the existence of racism or some other prejudice based on differences in ethnicity, class, gender, physical appearance, ability, or sexual orientation. Using techniques of story, such as sensory detail and dialogue, narrate your moment in time so that your audience can experience what you experi-

enced. Conclude your essay by reflecting on what you learned from your experience. What was the meaning of this event in your own life?

Positioning Pieces

The assignments in this category help students learn the importance of social location as a way of understanding diversity. Adrienne Rich, in her influential essay "Notes toward a Politics of Location" (1984, 212), defines the political nature of "position" or "location."

> As a woman I have a country; as a woman I cannot divest myself of that country merely by condemning its government. . . . I need to understand how a place on the map is also a place in history within which as a woman, a Jew, a lesbian, a feminist I am created and trying to create.

Rich notes that identity is a process of being created and creating. She argues that the process of "nam[ing] the ground we're coming from" means recognizing the privileges that one takes for granted, as well as the injustices one is attempting to fight. She notes, for instance, "I began to experience the meaning of my whiteness as a point of location for which I needed to take responsibility" (219). This acknowledgment of "position" is based on her recognition of the constructed nature of each person's frame of reference, the positional lens through which any given person sees the world. How positions get constructed is the focus of the positioning assignments in this section.

In our experience, minority students understand the concept of position more readily than do majority students, who often see their own experiences as transcendent or universal, and who therefore have little awareness that their "selves" have been socially constructed. Positioning assignments differ from narrative, autobiographical pieces in that they ask students to analyze multiple and conflicting elements of identity in a way that de-centers the self. These assignments immerse students in the tensions and complications of their own identities and invite each student to accept responsibility for his or her position in the world. At stake in these assignments is learning to present not an idealized autobiographical self who struggles with identity but a self defined by and in conflict with community.

One short positioning assignment used by Terri Hasseler relies on Peggy McIntosh's work in her essay "White Privilege and Male Privilege" (1992). McIntosh has constructed a list of ways in which white people, especially white men, experience privilege within U.S. culture. Her work is especially useful because it raises questions about the "hidden" forms of privilege that many people experience. Although McIntosh focuses on white and male privilege, an instructor can extend the discussion to other forms of privilege, such as educational and social class or physical appearance. Here is one way in which the assignment might be worded.

Example 7

> In class, we have been discussing Peggy McIntosh's views of privilege in U.S. culture. In a one-page, single-spaced thought letter, please reflect on how privilege, as defined by McIntosh and expanded on in our classroom discussion, has functioned (or not functioned) in your own life.

Through class discussion, students see that each kind of privilege is, itself, complexly layered. Educational privilege, for instance, needs to be contextualized in relation to the community the student came from (the percentage of people from their community or family who go to college), the community they have joined (whether a small liberal arts college, a community college, or an Ivy League college), and their means of support (whether scholarship, full- or part-time work, family contributions, or government assistance). Students thus learn to see their identity as a matrix filled with varying degrees of power and disempowerment.

The following positioning piece has been developed by Therese Saliba of Evergreen State College in Olympia, Washington.

Example 8

> Divide a piece of paper into three separate columns. In each column, answer the assigned question.
>
> Column 1: What terms would you use to define yourself?
> Column 2: What terms would friends, family members, teachers, coworkers, and other people who know you use to define you?
> Column 3: What words would someone who does not know you use to define you?

In reference to column 3, we suggest that instructors use a series of concrete examples to help students think through the ways they are constructed physically. For instance, instructors might ask, "How might a store employee in a large urban area, such as Detroit, define you?" or, "How might an attendant at an airline ticket counter in Bombay, New York, or Moscow describe you?"

It is stunning to note that students conditioned to be conscious of their ethnic or gender identities usually list those terms in all three columns. Most students, however, define themselves in terms that transcend ethnic or gender categories (e.g., "intellectual," "energetic," "bubbly"). Such students are often confused about what to write in the third column, whereas students who are conscious of themselves as being "seen" list their physically defining features there. Those less conscious of being "seen" resist thinking about how their physical appearance defines them and choose words like "nervous" ("I must be 'nervous' if I am in a different country"). But once they see the reality of their physical appearance, they become engaged with such questions as how class, education, economic position, ethnicity, gender, and age are physically reflected through the constructs of clothes, makeup, and body language. Moreover, students begin to discuss how they judge others all day long through clues based on physical appearance. In addition, imagining specific locations helps students learn that different global positions place them in differing complex relationships with power. Through classroom discussion, the stereotypical assumptions students might form about these locations can be investigated. The writing assignment that follows this classroom exercise is to compose a short, reflective essay addressing how physical appearance both constructs and hides the inner self.

A longer and more formal positioning assignment has been developed by Steve Clifford, an independent scholar. Clifford assigns readings on ethnic, religious, sexual, and biological identity and has the class view films and discuss popular images of diverse peoples in video games and advertising. The emphasis of the discussions and readings is to consider the ways in which labels position us in our world and the ways in which we can define ourselves according to positions we hold. He then gives the following assignment.

Example 9

> Choose and critically analyze a term of identity you use to define yourself or that other people use to define you, such as *Asian American, white, girl, boy, queer, jock,* and so forth. Your task is to make a claim about how your chosen term has been socially constructed through essays, advertising, and media (including film, news, and television) and about how its social construction has influenced the way you define yourself.

What has been particularly successful about Clifford's assignment is the way it helps students see how their personal sense of identity (what might be called the romanticized trope of the "authentic self") has been shaped by a larger cultural and social framework of conflict and power. This assignment also steers a middle ground between personal writing and academic argument. Students here control the degree of personal stories they wish to share and use them not as ends in themselves but as illustrations needed to support a thesis.

Ethnic Autobiographies

A final example of an inner-directed assignment asks students to construct their own ethnic autobiographies. University of Michigan sociologist David Schoem asks his students to write thirty- to fifty-page autobiographical papers prepared in stages throughout the term. The class develops a strict writing schedule, in which students complete roughly five pages of writing each week for the first half of the semester, when the focus is on idea generation. The second half of the semester focuses on revision, clarification, and reenvisioning. The style of writing is flexible, and the students often experiment with photo essays, collections of letters, interspersed poetry, and narrative. The text does not have to be a seamless narrative; it can be episodic, with unrelated chapters. (For details on how Schoem structures the assignment and integrates it with course content, consult Schoem 1991.)

Schoem's autobiography assignment has two purposes. First, it produces student texts to complement the professional course readings, which include Alice Walker and Sandra Cisneros; students' own lives and reflections become part of the course content. Second, student autobiographies create "an opportunity for students to discover for themselves the impact of [course] themes on their own lives and to recognize (at least for most) the degree of isolation and separation from others with whom they had lived their lives" (Schoem 1991, 11).

WORKS CITED

Bean, John C. 1996. *Engaging ideas: The professor's guide to integrating writing, critical thinking, and active learning in the classroom.* San Francisco: Jossey-Bass.

Belenky, Mary Field, Blythe McVicker Clinchy, Nancy Rule Goldberger, and Jill Mattick Tarule. 1986. *Women's ways of knowing: The development of self, voice, and mind.* New York: Basic.

Bleich, David. 1995. Collaboration and the pedagogy of disclosure. *College English* 57, no. 1:43–61.

Bridwell-Bowles, Lillian. 1992. Discourse and diversity: Experimental writing within the academy. *College Composition and Communication* 43, no. 3:349–68.

Britton, James, Tony Burgess, Nancy Martin, Alex McLeod, and Harold Rosen. 1975. *The development of writing abilities (11–18).* London: Macmillan.

Brown, J. E., ed. 1994. *SLATE* [Support for the Learning and Teaching of English]: *On intellectual freedom.* Urbana, IL: National Council of Teachers of English.

Flavell, John. H. 1963. *The developmental psychology of Jean Piaget.* New York: Van Nostrand.

Fox, Helen. 1994. *Listening to the world: Cultural issues in academic writing.* Urbana, IL: National Council of Teachers of English.

Goffman, Erving. 1979. *Gender advertisements.* New York: Harper and Row.

Hays, Janice N. 1983. The development of discursive maturity in college writers. In *The writer's mind: Writing as a mode of thinking,* ed. Janice N. Hays, P. A. Roth, R. R. Ramsey, and R. D. Foulke, 127–44. Urbana, IL: National Council of Teachers of English.

Kincaid, Jamaica. 1988. *A small place.* New York: Plume.

Krauthammer, Charles. 1988. How to save the homeless mentally ill. *New Republic,* 8 February, 22–25.

Lamb, Catherine E. 1991. Beyond argument in feminist composition. *College Composition and Communication* 42, no. 1:11–22.

McIntosh, Peggy. 1992. White privilege and male privilege: A personal accounting of coming to see correspondences through work in women's studies. In *Race, class, and gender: An anthology,* ed. Margaret L. Anderson and Patricia H. Collins, 70–81. Belmont, CA: Wadsworth.

Meisenhelder, S. 1985. Redefining "powerful" writing: Toward a feminist theory of composition. *Journal of Thought* 20:184–95.

Mirskin, Jerry. 1995. Writing as a process of valuing. *College Composition and Communication* 46, no. 3:387–410.

Nilson, L. B. 1997. Critical thinking as an exercise in courage. *National Teaching and Learning Forum* 6, no. 2:1–4.

Penrose, Ann, and Cheryl Geisler. 1994. Reading and writing without authority. *College Composition and Communication* 45, no. 4:505–20.

Perry, William G., Jr. 1970. *Forms of intellectual and ethical development in the college years: A scheme.* New York: Holt, Rinehart, and Winston.

Peterson, Linda H. 1991. Gender and the autobiographical essay: Research perspectives, pedagogical practices. *College Composition and Communication* 42, no. 2:170–83.

Ramage, John D., and John C. Bean. 2000. *The Allyn and Bacon guide to writing.* 2d ed. Needham Heights, MA: Allyn and Bacon.

Rich, Adrienne. 1984. Notes toward a politics of location. In *Blood, bread, and poetry,* 210–31. New York: Norton.

Rogers, Carl. 1961. *On becoming a person: A therapist's view of psychotherapy.* Boston: Houghton Mifflin.

Schoem, David, ed. 1991. *Inside separate worlds: Life stories of young Blacks, Jews, and Latinos.* Ann Arbor: University of Michigan Press.

Spellmeyer, Kurt. 1989. A common ground: The essay in the academy. *College English* 51, no. 3:262–76.

Swartzlander, Susan, Diana Pace, and Virginia Lee Stamler. 1993. The ethics of requiring students to write about their personal lives. *Chronicle of Higher Education* 17:B1–2.

Voss, J. F. 1989. On the composition of experts and novices. In *Thinking, reasoning, and writing,* ed. E. P. Maimon, B. F. Nodine, and F. W. O'Connor, 69–84. White Plains, NY: Longman.

Zeiger, William. 1985. The exploratory essay: Enfranchising the spirit of inquiry in college composition. *College English* 47, no. 5:454–66.

Chapter 7

Linking Assignment Design to Paper Grading in Classes about Diversity

Mark L. Waldo
University of Nevada, Reno
Reno, NV

Amanda Espinosa-Aguilar
Washington State University, Tri-Cities
Richland, WA

Grading papers has long been thought of as an onerous activity by students and faculty alike. Students have traditionally looked at grades on their papers, especially low grades, as subjective—based on instructor whim or prejudice or on some arbitrary standard left unexplained. Instructors themselves have perceived grading as too time-consuming, too distant from their own disciplines and experience, and sometimes too contentious, perpetuating unnecessary rifts between students and teachers.

While the grading of writing may have developed something of a bad reputation, the campuswide use of writing to enhance critical thinking in classes has acquired a very positive reputation. An increasing body of research demonstrates that this reputation is well deserved; writing about subject matter within courses assuredly improves a student's ability to remember, analyze, synthesize, categorize, and assert informed opinion about that subject matter (Langer and Applebee 1987; Hillocks 1986; Bazerman 1988). Good writing assignments place students at their zones of proximal development, challenging them cognitively without exceeding their limitations (Vygotsky 1979), helping them to move from dualistic thinking to relativism with commitment (Perry 1981). It stands to reason, then, that using writing, along with reading and discussion, would be a particularly effective way to promote diversity issues.

The University of Nevada, Reno (UNR), has adopted the premise that using writing helps students think about the material presented to them in class, and we have incorporated writing assignments focusing on diversity issues into our courses. Given UNR's student demographics, we believe we need such courses and writing assignments. UNR has a typical freshman population (99.4 percent are age twenty or younger), which is mostly Caucasian (87.5 percent) and largely (more than 70 percent) from middle-class and upper-middle-class economic backgrounds. Politically speaking, more than half of these freshmen describe themselves as either "middle-of-the-road" (29.8 percent) or "conservative or far right" (24.4 percent). This demography suggests that our students, particularly our freshmen, have not had much exposure to issues of diversity in the past or perhaps that our student body has been exposed to dualistic attitudes about issues of diversity. According to the academic master plan for UNR:

> . . . diversity is the opportunity to explore departures from traditional associations. It is a conscious movement into a world of both ideas and realities that may be different from accustomed experiences. Important aspects of diversity are appreciating cultural and gender differences within our own society, valuing global perspectives, and understanding the special needs of the disabled. (UNR 1996, 7)

To promote diversity, UNR has turned to its core curriculum courses, with freshman composition being among the most frequently designated, to introduce students to these new perspectives and learning experiences.

Promoting diversity is made possible by immersion, inclusion, revision, and revelation. For curricula to be diverse, they must reveal the inadequacies of existing canonical thought by including ideas, writings, and philosophies that have not been part of the traditional canon. As a result, bodies of knowledge are revised to represent a wider variety of thought and values. Immersion in this "new" arena can lead students toward pluralistic, tolerant thought, helping them recognize the impact of stereotypes and prejudices, as well as the sources of their own stereotypes and prejudices. It can help students to identify the differences between various cultural groups, as well as how attitudes and behaviors toward those groups are formed. Finally, such immersion opens students to theories and strategies that might make a shifting perspective possible.

Writing assignments may serve a central role in the immersion process. Of course, using writing in any class, including one on diversity, requires thinking about how that writing will be evaluated. Some writing may be assigned—journal responses, for example—with no intention of grading, but even then students will expect instructor comments. Perhaps students will assess each other's written work, with the instructor serving as arbiter. But most of the time (and this is true at UNR), the instructor will judge the quality of thinking and writing demonstrated in a piece—a judgment ordinarily manifesting itself in a grade. The question then becomes, How should writing be evaluated in courses promoting issues in cultural diversity, courses aligned with the goals we have outlined?

The problems with grading papers in other courses become amplified in courses on cultural diversity. There rarely are clear-cut answers to issues of race, gender, culture, or lifestyle choice. That answers are not clear-cut sometimes presents a disadvantage to graders because the accusation of subjectivity becomes more prominent. "My grade," students might readily proclaim, "comes from instructor bias toward this issue and not my response to it." To counter this charge, grading must be connected to the assignment itself.

For example, in a course exploring the impact of racial bias, an assignment might require that students examine existing affirmative action laws with regard to hiring within a local fire department. Instructors may assume that their grading would be based on how deeply and fairly their students examine both sides of the issue, using appropriate language and situations. For their part, students may have little beyond peripheral knowledge of affirmative action and may resort to unsubstantiated generalities or biased and inflamed opinion in their papers. If a paper's grade is lowered by the expression of generalities, bias, and narrow-mindedness (and most instructors would agree that it should be), students may then conceive of their grades as based on instructor prejudice. We argue that the opportunity for this sort of damaging confusion is lessened when assignments clearly lay out their requirements and when a paper's grade is based on how well it meets those requirements. We propose a grading environment that, based on criteria drawn from the assignments themselves, is at once efficient for instructors and safe and fair for student writers.

This chapter depends for its persuasiveness on readers accepting three related propositions. First, the ease, accuracy and fairness with which student papers are graded depends largely on the design of the assignment. Second, if instructors design their assignments with clear goals, engaging contexts, and identifiable audiences for writing, students will write better papers, and instructors will have better grading experiences. Third, the first two propositions are true for any classes, from those in physics to those on diversity issues. We have research to support these claims, drawn from our own experience and from the experience of others, both of which we will offer. But before we offer that research, we would like to explain what we mean by clear goals, engaging contexts, and identifiable audiences. We also want to assert that intervention with students as they write, when time allows, will markedly improve student performance.

Clear goals are the most important quality that writing assignments can have to enhance the writing and grading experience. All writing assignments have goals, whether explicitly stated or not. Some assignments ask students to write on topics of interest to them that have been discovered during the course of the term. Others are much more explicit in their expectations. For example, an instructor of English 102, "Issues in Cultural Diversity," might make the following assignment: "Write a paper (four to five pages) on a topic in cultural diversity (on race, gender, culture, or lifestyle choices) that interested you during the term." Alternatively, and preferably, the assignment might read: "Write a paper (four to five pages) examining the three most significant opposing points of view generated by the issue of providing health insurance to permanent partners in gay relationships. The paper must be balanced and well developed, without taking a position on the issue."

The first assignment offers no clear goal at all (except to write four to five pages on an issue in cultural diversity). It could develop into an argument, an analysis, a synthesis, or an examination of opposing points of view; it could develop into any expository task but, we contend, will probably end up being a very general treatment of a topic or topics, supported mainly by one or two research sources. When students do not know what the instructor expects from the assignment, the first thinking strategy they employ is trying to figure out what the instructor wants. Their second strategy is to "cover all the bases," by writing about everything in an effort to hit on something acceptable.

They often rely too much on their sources and too little on themselves, because sources seem safer than the expression and support of their own ideas. None of these strategies, however, is what instructors want or expect. Instructors view open-ended assignments as an opportunity to allow students the latitude to choose topics about which they can write the best papers, to use sources of their choice, and to organize according to a pattern they determine—all admirable goals.

Unfortunately, these admirable motivations lead too often to poor results. Open-ended assignments, without instructor intervention in topic selection or essay revision, omit essential information that most lower-division (and many upper-division) students need to write successfully. When students write the open-ended assignment, most do not know what they are supposed to be writing about. They struggle with selecting a topic, often choosing topics too broad to be covered within page limitations; they write in unsupported generalizations and overuse sources (or plagiarize); they grapple with organizational patterns dictated by the broadness of the topic or the research sources they have selected. They more readily slip into stereotyped, biased, and dualistic thinking in their papers. Often, because of fear and embarrassment, they refuse to ask questions in class or to go in for conferences with the instructor.

When writing on assignments with clear goals, in contrast, students begin by knowing what outcome the teacher is looking for. They think critically about the questions the assignment poses, not the assignment itself. They cannot, with success, rely on stereotypical and biased impressions to support their position. They organize according to specific parameters. If they have questions of the instructor, they know which ones to ask, because they are aware of the goals for the assignment.

Ironically, open-ended assignments (e.g., "Write on an issue of interest to you in cultural diversity") often lack the information teachers need to grade fairly and efficiently. Grading becomes an arbitrary activity, which requires the grader to interpret each paper's goals, decide how well those goals are met, and justify the decision by explaining, usually in the end comment, the grade for the paper. Teachers themselves may, under these conditions, accidentally slip into biased assessment.

If, however, the goal for the assignment is clear (i.e., to represent opposing points of view on the issue of health insurance for partners in gay relationships), students know that they must, to succeed, give analytic attention to arguments on both sides of the issue, without taking a side. For their part, graders know that they are looking for how well the students' representations reflect the depth and balance of their thinking. The design of the assignment itself helps instructors create criteria for grading, which increases fairness and efficiency. In other words, specifying goals presents advantages not only for students as writers but for teachers as graders.

Along with clear goals, effective assignments also provide students with an engaging context, locating them in some pertinent situation in which to write. In the case of the assignment about health insurance for partners in gay relationships, students may be placed in the position of arbitrators between management and those seeking such insurance; they may see themselves as siblings to an employee (heterosexual or homosexual) who is having difficulty accepting management's point of view; or they may write as consultants to a legislative body that is considering action on the issue. Perhaps the context becomes the classroom itself: the assignment might read, "Assume a division in thinking about the issue in your class; help those on each side understand the issue's complexity and implications." Each one of these situations will affect how writers think about the assignment—its content, its organization, and pertinent sources. As an important qualifier, we believe context and goals should engage students at their levels of interest and preparation. Freshmen will probably not excel at writing on topics appropriate for seniors, and seniors will probably not be challenged by topics more pertinent to freshmen. Each assignment should stretch students cognitively, without exceeding their abilities, and should encourage them to work together to solve the problems the assignment poses.

Lastly, we propose that assignments offer an identifiable audience that the writer sees as clearly related to the assignment's context. In the case of the assignment on insurance for partners in gay relationships, students might write to employees and management, to siblings, to legislative bodies, to each other, or to their teachers. Writing to specific audiences helps students develop a sense of the shape and tone of their essays. To illustrate, imagine students writing to persuade an ambivalent audience (perhaps management), those who have not formed an opinion about health insurance for partners in gay relationships. As writers supporting or refuting such insurance, students understand that they have a chance to convince this audience because of its ambivalence. But they could not do so without carefully considering their tone, which would need to be moderate and reflective, or their organizational strategy, which would place a charitable and thoughtful refutation of their opponents' point of view before a complete explanation of their own position. With regard to grading, students who adopt an emphatic tone would alienate this audience, while those who adopt a reflective and moderate tone would embrace it, and each could be evaluated accordingly. To substantiate our point, we want to step away from the arena of cultural diversity for a few pages, because we assert that the principles for grading papers remain the same in all classes.

The advantages to grading papers with clear goals, engaging contexts, and specific audiences become evident through looking at an assignment made in an introductory physics course.

> You go out to the mailbox one day, where you receive the following letter from your younger brother:
>
> > Dear Pat: You sent your younger brother a bum recipe. Either you Reno people don't know what a good soft-boiled egg is, or you made a mistake in your last letter to me. In New York, a three-minute egg is cooked for three minutes. So how come you cook your "three-minute eggs" for a longer time? Come on, is the boiling water colder in Reno? (Ha, ha—that's a joke!) Please explain to me what is going on.
>
> Write a letter to your brother (three to five pages) explaining why you have to cook "three-minute eggs" for longer than three minutes in Reno. He's a bright kid, but he hasn't had a college physics course. Don't try to smoke him with textbook jargon. Just explain to him in clear language what is going on. In your letter, discuss such features as (1) the relationship of atmospheric pressure to altitude, (2) the effect of pressure on boiling point, (3) the relationship of the heat content of water to boiling point, and (4) the transfer of heat from the water to the egg. (Adapted from a physics assignment created by Larry Kirkpatrick, Physics Department, Montana State University)

Because the following criteria are included as part of the assignment, students know they will be graded on (1) the accuracy of their explanations; (2) the clarity, development, and completeness of their explanations; (3) the appropriateness of their explanations for someone the brother's age; and (4) the overall effectiveness of their writing style. This assignment poses a very interesting (and cognitively challenging) problem for students in an introductory physics class. It gives them an engaging context: nearly a mile above sea level, the eggs *would* take longer to boil. And it supplies an audience: a bright but uninformed brother to whom textbook jargon would be abhorrent. These qualities make possible the best writing experience for students.

The inclusion of goals, context, and audience also make papers written on such an assignment as this the best experience to grade. When there is such clarity, graders know what to expect and can evaluate papers according to the degree that they find the required features. We support this claim by describing the results of more than twenty paper-grading sessions that personnel from UNR's Writing Center have conducted with faculty. During these sessions, instructors read five student papers written from Kirkpatrick's physics assignment and ranked them from most successful to least successful, offering reasons for their ranking, then sharing their rankings and reasons with their colleagues. Faculty almost uniformly agreed on which papers constitute top, middle, and bottom papers. This agreement occurred whether those participating in the sessions were faculty in natural sciences, social sciences, professional schools, humanities, or education. Further, faculty averaged ten minutes to read and rank each paper. We attribute the agreement and shortness of reading time largely to the quality of the assignment itself. Our point, however, is not to pretend that assignments in physics are the same as assignments in courses emphasizing cultural diversity. They are not. Instead, we wish to emphasize how grading is enhanced by the clarity of the assignment itself, as well as how such clarity may be achieved in both types of classes.

Further evidence supporting the merits of focused assignment making comes from evaluating ten papers on each of two different assignments in upper-division criminal justice classes. The first, assigned in a junior-level course on juvenile justice, required students to write five to seven pages, due at term's end, on a topic of interest to them discovered during the semester. The second, also assigned in a junior-level course—criminal justice administration—required that students argue for their own promotion in a criminal justice agency at which they have worked 3.5 years. Their promotion paper must draw from Machiavelli's *The Prince,* presenting, according to the assignment, "their philosophies in three general areas: the assumption of authority, personnel administration, and financial administration (which, by sheer coincidence, could be construed as the three primary subject areas of *The Prince*)." As another "sheer coincidence," the supervisor evaluating the students' applications has written her master's thesis on *The Prince.* However, states the assignment, "you need not be totally positive and should feel free to disagree with Machiavelli where necessary" (adapted from an assignment created by Ken Peak, Criminal Justice Department, UNR). The criteria for grading the second assignment were based on how well students set forth their administrative position; the extent to which they weave in Machiavelli's views (pro and con), thereby demonstrating that they have read and understood the book; and their ability to communicate that information to the supervisor by being clear, concise, and accurate.

Because there are no stated expectations for the first assignment (beyond writing five to seven pages on topics of interest in juvenile justice), the readers reviewing these papers (four criminal justice faculty and two consultants from the Writing Center in 1995) had a very difficult time evaluating them. Goals for each of the papers and the degree to which each writer met the goals were matters of reader interpretation and preference, creating jumbled rankings and pronounced disagreements. Deciding what constituted top, middle, and bottom papers was impossible, because readers could not establish uniform criteria by which to judge them. Reading each of the papers took committee members twenty to thirty minutes; presumably, the instructor took longer, because of the need to make notes in the text to point to numerous problems and to offer closing comments to justify the grade. Characterized by topics too broad and complex for the length required, the majority of the papers were flaccid and unfocused, overused outside sources, and included many sentence-level problems. The readers agreed that only four of the papers would "succeed" in any minimal sense of the word and that six of the ten would receive a letter grade of D or F.

In contrast, the assignment using *The Prince* produced papers that nearly uniformly succeeded, with nine out of ten receiving letter grades of A or B from reviewers. Each of these papers took the six readers under ten minutes to read and evaluate. The instructor confirmed this assessment, claiming that an astonishing ninety out of one hundred students did receive A or B grades and that each paper took under ten minutes to read, comment on, and grade. The difference in success rates between these sets of papers supports the findings of George Hillocks (1986, 247), whose research in composition determined that paper assignments with clear and specific objectives produce markedly better writing than do paper assignments without those objectives.

Even with less-than-clear goals, assignments can be made better through teacher intervention with students during the process of writing. Examples of intervention include conferences between student and instructor, focused small-group work with peers, or comments on drafts followed by revision. If the purpose of the intervention is to help students limit and shape topics, then obviously faculty should talk to students as they are considering their topics, before they begin to write. This type of one-on-one talk would have helped students writing the first criminal justice paper. It would also have helped the instructor to grade the papers. Knowing the goals the students had chosen for writing, the instructor could then have based grading on how well they met those goals.

Intervening after students draft their papers but before they turn them in for grading also has a positive impact, because students can make changes between their rough draft and their final copy. Hillocks's experiment with hundreds of student writers indicated "that focused comments coupled with . . . revision" produced far better results than did writing comments on final drafts without the option of revision: "The gain for students doing revision (1.57) was nearly twice that for students receiving comments but doing no revision (.89)" (Hillocks 1986, 167). This means that if faculty take the time to put comments on the papers they receive from students (and most do), doing so on rough drafts while students still have time to make changes produces far better results than does waiting until the final copy, which produces no discernible improvement on future papers.

Our own confirmation of the claim of improvement between draft and final copy comes from Writing Center work with electrical engineering faculty (Waldo, Blumner, and Webb 1995) while they evaluated the writing of their upper-division students. Readers from the electrical engineering committee for writing assessment (two electrical engineers and two consultants from the Writing Center) agreed that instructor feedback during the process of writing led to markedly better results than did merely grading and returning papers. They found six of seven papers drawn from a 400-level course in digital systems, for example, to be of nearly "publishable" quality, largely (they later agreed) because of the instructor's semester-long readings of, and focused comments on, drafts. Less dramatic but nonetheless very positive results were achieved on lab reports written for integrated circuit engineering, where eight of ten papers succeeded at A or B grade levels. The instructor for the lab read and commented on (orally or in writing) drafts of all these reports.

Our discussion thus far has laid the groundwork for principles to guide grading. We have stressed that the grading experience, positive or negative, depends largely on the quality of the assignment and the opportunity to work with students as they write. At this point, we want to describe assignments and grading in Dr. Espinosa-Aguilar's English 102 course, centered on the theme of multiculturalism. Importantly, we are not describing a class in which the student population is diverse (recall the demographics of UNR's freshman class). Instead, we are describing a class whose writing and reading assignments centered on issues of diversity.

Seven essay assignments, ranging from whether students viewed the movement for political correctness as positive to if they had any experiences with bigotry, were composed for the English 102 class. Many of the assignments produced essays and grading experiences that support the claims we have asserted about grading. Dr. Espinosa-Aguilar found that the quality of writing and grading was directly linked to the design of the assignment and to her opportunity for teacher intervention. Two of her assignments, one unsuccessful and the other successful, illustrate these points.

The unsuccessful assignment was the second one students wrote for the course. It required students to use various sources to determine whether UNR was truly multicultural in its course offerings or merely providing token classes. Since her research interests lie within multicultural studies, Dr. Espinosa-Aguilar had a hidden purpose in assigning the topic, although she did not tell her students that at the time. She wanted to find out which majors students thought offered the largest number of diversity-oriented courses; she did not believe any of them did. To this end, she made the following assignment.

> Using the UNR catalog and our text, write an essay in which you argue whether UNR offers diverse and multicultural classes. I'd suggest looking at maybe one major (possibly your own) to make this determination. Do not use the class schedule alone. Look at the catalog to see what the university claims it offers in terms of diversity classes, then look at any campus activities or requirements that might also prove or disprove your case.

Dr. Espinosa-Aguilar mistakenly believed that the assignment was clear in its goals. This assignment, however, was far from clear. The essays were almost uniformly disappointing, and her experience grading them was grueling.

Dr. Espinosa-Aguilar had high hopes that the essays written on this assignment would reveal to her students the lack of diversity that she already believed existed in the UNR curriculum. Having looked over the materials herself, she expected students to confirm her conclusion that the university generally failed to include traditionally underrepresented groups in the curriculum and thus that it sent a message, perhaps unintentionally, that diversity was not important enough to teach or study. She also assumed that once her students saw these inadequacies in the curriculum, they would want it revised so that they could take alternative courses that allowed them to examine different cultures, races, genders, and traditions. Evidently, the hidden purpose did not reveal itself to her students. They assumed that she thought the university curriculum was already diverse, and they wrote from their assumption that she wanted to hear that university offerings taught students the values of multicultural thinking.

Examining this assignment makes it clear why the students produced the essays they did and why the instructor had such a hard time grading them. First, the wording of the main goal for the assignment confused the students. A major problem occurred from her use of the term *diverse* instead of *diversity-oriented.* Many students looked at this goal and, given the large number of classes offered in the catalog and schedule, concluded immediately that there was a diversity of classes offered all of the time. Students too often focused on the definition of *diverse* as "many in number," not "varied in culture." The instructor's lack of attention to word choice in designing this assignment added significantly to the difficulty students had in drafting their essays and, consequently, to her difficulty in grading them. Even though assignment terminology may seem like a small issue, it should not be taken lightly. The misuse of one word can obscure the goals of an entire assignment.

Because students often did not meet other requirements of the assignment as well, it took the instructor longer to grade the papers, because she had to justify grades with end comments explaining what the students did not do. The assignment asks the students to consider using their major as a source for their essays; often students did not do this because, as freshmen, they had not chosen majors. The assignment asks them to use the textbook, catalog, and class schedule; none of the students used all three (in fact, none used the schedule), and few used them as was hoped—as evidence revealing the diversity offerings in the curriculum. It became clear that most students did not yet know how to read and cite these texts as evidence. Few students looked at how student organizations influence diversity on campus, because they did not know about such organizations or how, beyond the obvious, those organizations impact the inclusion of diversity. Because of the students' failures to meet her vague assignment requirements in their essays, Dr. Espinosa-Aguilar struggled with her evaluations of their papers.

Since the goals for the assignment were not specific (particularly the goal to survey diversity offerings by major), the students resorted to second-guessing the "real purpose" of the assignment. Perhaps the largest contributor to this second-guessing was the instructor's failure to admit her unexpressed goal for the assignment: to reveal the curriculum as lacking. Repeatedly, the students resorted to broad conclusions, including the generality that university education is the panacea for solving problems related to diversity. A number of essays, for example, included fallacies and clichés about the value of education for eradicating racism. Unexpressed goals, along with broadly unmanageable ones, ultimately led these students to offer unsupported opinions that they thought the professor wanted to hear. The open-ended nature of this assignment also resulted in essays that lacked authentic contexts and audiences. Students did not know to whom they were writing (university officials? peers? the professor herself?) or why (to analyze? to synthesize? to persuade?), and they demonstrated no personal commitment to the notion of teaching classes devoted to cultural issues. All of these faults made grading a nightmare; Dr. Espinosa-Aguilar arbitrarily graded the papers based on which essays most nearly met her original intentions, though few did. She struggled with end comments, marginalia, and letter grades—perceiving that because of the quality of the assignment, she may have been grading herself.

In retrospect, the professor believes that the students would have written better papers if she had used conferences and peer groups to clarify the assignment and to help with context, the use of sources, organization, and audience. She did use such techniques while students wrote the next assignment, which itself was far clearer in goals, context, and audience.

> I want you to consider how sexism has affected your world. Write an essay that re-creates specific experiences of sexism you have encountered. You should use interviews, anecdotes, and textual evidence to show why sexism remains a problem in your life. Then draw conclusions from your experience that determine whether you believe sexism is still a problem in American society. Think about writing this to other freshmen who may not recognize sexism's effect on their own lives.

This assignment has a clear goal: to reveal to students how sexism has affected their world. It has an engaging context, which immerses the students in the issues at a level appropriate to their cognitive abilities. It offers an audience: freshmen who may not have thought much about their own experience of sexism. These features, by themselves, set this assignment apart from the earlier one.

The chance for intervention set it further apart. When the instructor had the opportunity to confer with each student (twice), the papers generally became better, since the students revised according to specific directions. During these private conferences, Dr. Espinosa-Aguilar modeled the kinds of questions to ask that would enable students to clarify their goals, audience, and contexts during large- and small-group discussions in class. These discussions allowed students to talk through ideas and ask their peers for advice. They also prompted students to practice drawing conclusions from evidence that supported their ideas. Consequently, the students did an effective job of implementing, analyzing, and commenting on the quotes put into their essays. Students did not look for easy answers and conclusions; they were willing to let their writing honestly reflect the ways that sexism operated in their world, even if it meant ending the paper on a negative note—that is, acknowledging that sexism remains a persistent problem.

Grading the essays on sexism took very little time, due to the initial clarity of the assignment and to the opportunity for intervention during the drafting process. Students knew that their grades would be lowered if fallacies, gross generalizations, and lack of analysis were evident in their essays. They also knew that high-scoring essays would reflect specific personal experience, effective quoting, original thinking, and peer audience. They knew that grades would be based not on opinion but on how well each student met the assignment's criteria. Since the sexism essay was not designed with any hidden agenda (beyond one hidden even from Dr. Espinosa-Aguilar herself), the students did not have to second-guess what the instructor would be looking for when she went to evaluate their assignments. They knew what she expected and gave it to her in original and engaging ways.

When instructors assign essays that deal with issues of diversity, they need to consider what their grades may imply to their students. Regardless of their backgrounds, students often think that teachers grade on opinions and that the grade reflects the student's ability to give back to the teacher what has been put forward all semester long. The sexism assignment illustrates this point; it inadvertently insists, as a requirement, that "sexism remains a problem in [students' lives]." Students faced with this assignment may rightly think that they must describe personal experiences of sexism, whether they believe they have had them or not, or risk getting a lower or even failing grade. Dr. Espinosa-Aguilar did not intend to force her students into this situation (this was the agenda hidden even to her). In fact, she thinks that lowering her students' grades because of their experience (or lack of it) is unethical. During the conversations in class and in conference, she broadened the topic to allow for students who claimed not to have experienced sexism, thus demonstrating that intervention can alleviate unanticipated problems.

Dr. Espinosa-Aguilar's testimony from her class supports our earlier claims. Carefully designed assignments produce better writing and deeper thinking than do open-ended assignments. When these focused assignments are coupled with student conferences, instructors may expect to generate very positive results. Other conclusions are also probable. First, though by no means advocating poorly designed assignments, we assert that conferences by themselves will lessen the negative effects of such assignments, because conferences give students the opportunity to ask questions about goals and criteria for grading and provide teachers the opportunity to clarify their expectations and to help shape the students' papers accordingly. Second, if there is little or no time for conferences, focused assignments will lead to markedly better writing than will open-ended assignments. Third, regardless of conferencing, focused assignments make grading papers a much more efficient and equitable process.

We want to add, as we close, a few other practical points about grading papers. First, if instructors are going to put end comments and marginalia on papers, they serve the grading process and their students better by doing so on rough drafts, not final copies. Students will then have the opportunity to apply the comments to writing final drafts. If this seems too radical a departure from traditional practice to entertain, we suggest that closing comments on final copies be limited to two points: (1) the paper's single greatest strength and (2) the paper's most important area for improvement—given the assignment's parameters. By writing more, instructors risk losing their own focus and the student's attention. Using the sexism assignment for an example, assume that John B. does a good job of developing an essay about his experience with sexism: he uses anecdotes, interviews, and textual evidence; and he clearly addresses his essay to his freshman peers. Assume that John B. does not, however, draw more general conclusions about sexism remaining a problem in American society. The instructor's end comment would then reflect those qualities in John B.'s essay: for example, "You've done a fine job of demonstrating sexism in your life with engaging examples, anecdotes, the interview, and the evidence you've chosen. An area for improvement would be to show how sexism remains a problem in American society generally." Such a comment makes clear what the instructor/grader finds in the essay, as well as what she does not find.

A second, related suggestion is to limit sentence-level correction to the one or two errors most prominently disruptive to the communication of the paper's points. To correct more (or to correct everything) is to risk having students focus shallowly on the whole and deeply on nothing. Assume that John B. includes in his essay several fragmented sentences and numerous comma errors, which distract the reader. Assume that his essay also includes some inappropriate tense shifts and errors in pronoun and subject/verb agreement but that these are far fewer and do not inhibit communication. The pertinent editorial response would be to point out and correct the fragmented sentences and commas, alerting the writer to the communicative problems and advising him to watch for those problems next time.

A third suggestion is to describe criteria in advance for papers receiving A, B, C, or lower grades. Describing criteria in advance helps instructors to clarify their expectations for themselves and helps students to understand those expectations as they write. Again using the sexism essay as an example, we suggest that Dr. Espinosa-Aguilar might delineate the following criteria. Assuming that sexism exists in the students' lives, grading might be explained as follows.

- An A paper will use sharply focused, relevant personal experiences to demonstrate sexism in your life; it will ably integrate anecdotes, interviews, and textual evidence in support of its point; it will move convincingly from the individual to the general in establishing sexism as a continuing societal problem; it will include few, if any, sentence-level problems; and its tone, diction, and syntax will clearly address peers.
- A B paper will also use relevant personal experiences, but they may not be so sharply focused as those in the A paper; a B paper will integrate anecdotes, interviews, and evidence, but perhaps not so ably as in the A paper; a B paper will move from the individual to the general, but with less coherence and conviction than occurs in the A paper; it may include more sentence-level problems than the A paper, though they will not interfere with the communication of ideas; and its tone, diction, and syntax, while appropriate to its audience, may not be so conscious of it as in the A paper.
- A C paper will meet each of the principal requirements of the assignment, but with less facility and coherence than demonstrated in the A or B papers; or it may not address one or more of the requirements at all but do well on others.
- D or F papers will be correspondingly weaker in any or all areas.

Graders will of course adjust their expectations as they read the papers, weighing or not weighing requirements as they perceive their students responding to the assignment. Perhaps the instructor/grader might randomly select and read five papers in advance, establishing levels of quality into which the remaining papers may fit.

Because diversity deals with heated issues, it is imperative to evaluate papers fairly and sensitively, based on criteria the students recognize as linked directly to the assignment and the class and not to their experience. We would recommend, nonetheless, that papers be read and evaluated for the whole of their success and not be scored numerically by their parts. If a goal of diversity classes is to stimulate acceptance of other cultures, languages, literatures, or ways of thinking, how many students will be accepting when they receive a 72 out of 100? Numbers pretend to objectify what cannot, in the case of papers on diversity issues, be objectified; and quantifying the demonstration of diverse thinking would seem antithetical to encouraging it.

WORKS CITED

Bazerman, Charles. 1988. *Shaping written knowledge.* Madison: University of Wisconsin Press.

Hillocks, George, Jr. 1986. *Research on written composition.* Urbana, IL: National Council of Teachers of English.

Langer, Judith, and Arthur Applebee. 1987. *How writing shapes thinking.* Urbana, IL: National Council of Teachers of English.

Perry, William, Jr. 1981. Cognitive and ethical growth: The making of meaning. In *The modern American college,* ed. Arthur Chickering and Associates. San Francisco: Jossey-Bass.

University of Nevada, Reno. 1996. *Approaching the twenty-first century: Academic master plan for 1997–2001, University of Nevada, Reno.* Reno: University and Community College System of Nevada.

Vygotsky, Lev. 1979. *Mind in society.* Ed. Michael Cole, Vera John-Steiner, Sylvia Scribner, and Ellen Souberman. Cambridge: Harvard University Press.

Waldo, Mark L., Jacob Blumner, and Mary Webb. 1995. Writing centers and writing assessment: A discipline-based approach. In *Writing center perspectives,* ed. Eric Hobson, Christina Murphy, and Bryon Stay. Emmitsburg, MD: NWCA Press.

Chapter 8

Out of the Closet: Writing to Learn

Steven Hartwell
University of San Diego
San Diego, CA

Introduction

In a world in which destructive distinctions based on race, sex, and socioeconomic class are now thought to reflect only social ignorance, homophobia remains a glaring example of intolerance. An "educated" person who would not think of disparaging another on the basis of race, religion, or sex might disparage homosexuals. For those of us for whom teaching entails a commitment to creating a safer and healthier world, nothing can be more important than helping to liberate students from this pernicious form of ignorance.

In this chapter, I relate my teaching experience using experiential classroom teaching methods combined with certain writing techniques that may help students deal more openly with issues of homosexuality. I place these exercises within a framework of learning and ethical theory.

Word Usage

One of the important things I have learned from my teaching experience has been to clarify my word usage. In this chapter, I refer to women whose primary sexual attraction is other women with the term *lesbians* and to men whose primary attraction is other men with the term *gay*. I use the term *straight* nonpejoratively to refer to heterosexual men and women. I do not ordinarily use the term *homosexual* as an adjective, unless it seems the easiest fit. I use the term *gay* to emphasize the socially constructed, cultural aspects of the lives of gay men and lesbians somewhat in the same way *gender* describes the social construction of sexuality. Genes and genitalia determine one's sex, but society informs one's gender (Money 1980). Roy Cohn and J. Edgar Hoover were both (reputedly) homosexual men, but I do not think of them as "gay," because they were not part of gay culture. (The lines blurred when Cohn posthumously became a "gay" character in the hit play *Angels in America*.) In contrast, Bette Midler and the late Judy Garland, both straight, are members of gay culture because their dramatic characters resonate with so many gay men.

Queer is a more problematic term. Historically, it was a term of derision, like *fag*. *Fag* remains insulting, but *queer* now occupies a special place in gay lexicon, to denote, typically, the radicalness or "otherness" of the gay experience. In describing itself, for example, gay literary criticism is likely to employ the adjective *queer*.

Genes may influence one's sexual orientation (i.e., to whom one is attracted), but society informs how that attraction is lived out and how it is talked about. Some recent research suggests that male homosexuality may be genetically influenced but that female sexuality is not (Hamer and Copeland 1998). My sole interest in this chapter is helping students respond in healthy ways to the fact of homosexuality.

The terms *out* and *closeted* refer to whether one's homosexuality is known to others or not. These two terms are always relative, because only a few gays are totally "closeted" in the sense that their sexual orientation is known to no one, and typically only gay celebrities, like k.d. lang or Ellen DeGeneres, are "out" to nearly everyone. For most gays, "coming out" is an ongoing process in which they must decide with whom, on what occasions, and for what reasons to reveal their sexual orientation. I use these terms in accordance with the gay community with which I am most familiar.

Later in this chapter, I use the term *experiential* in two slightly different ways that I hope will be clear through context. I use *experiential* to describe any teaching method that employs a "hands-on" approach, such as role plays, journals, quick writes, field placements, and so forth. *Experiential* is also the term employed by Seymour Epstein (1994) and other educational psychologists to describe a modality of knowing associated with feeling that Epstein distinguishes from a second, more verbal, "rational" modality of knowing associated with intellectual ideas. The two meanings can be easily confused, because something one learns through an experiential teaching method, such as learning about one's own sexuality through an interactive role play, is likely to then be known by that person not only rationally but affectively in the knowing modality Epstein calls experiential.

Organization of the Chapter

The first part of this chapter looks at how we learn about sexuality in early childhood and its influence on how we think and write about sexuality in later life. I there closely examine early-childhood learning, not only because most of our fundamental ideas about sexuality are learned very early in life, but because most of us treat this kind of early learning differently from learning acquired later in life. The things we learn about in early life, such as sex and food, have a special kind of robustness and status that we do not accord to things learned later in life. Understanding how this early learning differs from later learning helps explain the resistance of many students to writing or thinking rationally about homosexuality. The second part of this chapter provides a theoretical basis, as well as an ethical analysis, for the use of writing that helps students think about homosexuality more rationally. The third part of this chapter builds on the first two by introducing classroom exercises that may help broaden student attitudes about gay sexuality and, thereby, enlarge their capacity to think and write about it.

Writing and Thinking

A major, stated premise of the writing-to-learn literature is that writing is a form of thinking (Zinsser 1988). An often unstated but implied premise is that this "thinking" is essentially a cognitive process encompassing logical analysis, clarity, order, and plausibility and taking place within a context of cultural values. Yet writing is also an affective process through which writers access the moods and feelings that color and shape the thinking they wish to express. Good writing synthesizes the cognitive with the affective so that the reader experiences such writing as coherent.

Sometimes feelings impede writing (Davis and Schwartz 1987). A colleague of mine who quite casually agreed to write a brief essay on the Holocaust discovered that the act of writing it plunged her into such intense feelings that she initially could not write. Even many years after the event, another colleague, because of her intense feelings of loss, can communicate only guardedly about her infant daughter who lived only a few days.

Taboo Topics

My interest in writing this chapter concerns one variation in which feelings impede thinking and writing. This variation concerns certain themes or topics, such as homosexuality, that I call "taboo topics." Taboo topics entail three characteristics that distinguish them from the emotional blocks my two colleagues encountered. First, not only are students unable to think rationally about a taboo topic, but they cannot address their incapacity to think about it. For reasons I will explain, I call this incapacity to think about "the unthinkable" a "metarule." Second, a taboo is typically learned so early in childhood that the student currently experiences the taboo as "natural," though it is in fact something she or he once learned. This early-childhood learning that seems later to simply be "natural" comprises what I label the "yuck test." Third, a taboo is culturally supported and maintained. In the case of the taboo about homosexuality, this cultural support is sometimes called the "heterosexual bias."

Taboos as Metarules: Rules against Knowing

A significant difficulty educators face in trying to help students engage their taboos is that thinking about the taboo topic is, itself, typically taboo. In the words of R. D. Laing, there are "rules against knowing about certain rules" (Laing 1971, 111). Not only does the student have a rule that something is not to be thought about (homosexuality), but there is a further rule that no such rule exists. Hence, if the student were asked, "Is there a reason that you cannot even think about homosexuality?" the student might respond, "No, there is not"—before promptly changing the subject. A taboo thus acts as a "metarule" in that it functions as a rule about other rules. The metarule not only keeps students from thinking about homosexuality but also represses their examining why they cannot think about it. Because the learning took place so early in childhood, the students do not know they have learned a metarule.

Part 1: How We Learn about Sexuality

Early-Childhood Learning and the "Yuck Test"

Early-childhood learning differs qualitatively from how we learn as adults. Early-childhood learning is tacit, typically entailing little or no language. Because there is so little language involved, the young child learns directly and uncritically from experience, without the mediating effect of words. Consider how a very young child learns to distinguish between food and nonfood. Imagine, for example, a one- or two-year-old boy. The mother offers him something new, such as applesauce. The mother smacks her lips, smiles, nods, makes such comments as "Mmm, this is yummy for your tummy," and spoons forward the applesauce. The little boy squirms in eager anticipation. He tests it out and, with a little luck, does find it yummy. An hour later, out in the garden, he finds a snail and an oleander leaf and contemplates tasting them. His mother lets out a shriek, grimaces, and says, "No, ugh, yucky snail! Yucky oleander!" The frightened infant now has been etched for life with something approaching absolute certitude, supported by a powerful affective reaction, that snails and oleander are not simply "nonfood" but disgusting and perhaps dangerous as well. Twenty years later, he will not only continue to find revolting the notion of even thinking about eating snails and oleander but, more importantly, he will be convinced that this notion is natural.

The Little Boy Grows Up

Later in life, our little boy may travel to France and encounter people who find escargot not only edible but delicious. He may also learn, at some point, that in no culture do people eat oleander, because oleander is indeed poisonous. He may intellectually conclude that there is no accounting for taste and that people are entitled to eat what they want, but he will never lose the feeling that snails and oleander are disgusting and that people who eat such things have something wrong with them. Intellectually he distinguishes between cultural choice and health, but emotionally he does not. For him, both snails and oleander meet the "yuck" litmus test.

During childhood, our same little boy probably learned the fundamentals of sexuality in basically the same way he learned about food and nonfood. We know, through such researchers as Colwyn Trevarthen (1995), that toddlers know their gender by eighteen months of age and gender-appropriate behavior before three years. They learn identification essentially nonverbally and often in ways, such as through teasing, that carry a great deal of affect. Two-year-old children already have rules that prescribe much harsher treatment for gender-deviant boys ("sissies") than for gender-deviant girls ("tomboys"). Children make distinctions about gender-appropriate behavior even before they are able to distinguish between boys and girls on the basis of anatomy (Bem 1993). Boys learn at a very early age that being "sissy" or "queer"—whatever the terms may mean to them—is particularly shameful.

The Little Boy Grows up Differently from the Little Girl

The distinction between how boys and girls learn about sexuality growing up is important. While growing up, little boys suffer two significant disadvantages that affect their adult understanding of sexuality. First, their gender roles are much more restrictive than those of girls. Usually, a girl can happily be a "tomboy" and aspire to be a firefighter, but a boy cannot happily be a "sissy" and aspire to be a preschool teacher. Girls can sometimes be tough, but boys can never be soft. Girls are permitted a greater range of expression than boys. Sexuality, like art, literature, and play, is a process through which one's whole personality can be expressed. A man who has a more restricted self-concept of what his gender permits him to be and do has a more restricted range in expressing his sexuality. Second, girls typically identify with their mothers as their primary caretakers, but boys must learn to separate from their mothers if they are to become men.

Liam Hudson and Bernadine Jacot, in their book *The Way Men Think: Intellect, Intimacy, and Erotic Imagination* (1991), offer a brilliant analysis of the separation pain boys may suffer emotionally and psychologically in leaving their mothers. The authors call the hurt inflicted on boys from their premature separation, a separation that occurs in the boys' first few years, the "male wound." As a result of this wound, men typically learn as infants to fear intimacy and loss of sexual control. Prostitution and pornography may primarily attract men because they permit men to control their sexuality and to avoid intimacy. For many men, thoughts of homoerotic intimacy are extraordinarily threatening. Such thoughts threaten a man's need to remain in control as well as his narrowly defined understanding of what it means sexually to be a man. In my teaching experience, virtually all of the students for whom thinking rationally about homosexuality is taboo are males. Most of the journal writings I receive from students about gay issues come from women; when men do write about gay issues, they often write about their difficulties in addressing the topic or their sadness in abandoning a childhood friend when they discovered the friend was gay.

My Own Early Learning

My own early experience may be instructive here and may resonate with other male readers. I remember being with my mother at a movie theater when I was about four years old. She sent me unaccompanied, most likely for the first time, to the public men's room. She warned me, with an intensity I have never forgotten, that I was not to talk to anyone there. At that age, though I had only the most rudimentary factual knowledge of sex, I did have some undifferentiated, mostly physical feeling that linked gender with the pleasant feelings of dropping one's pants and urinating. The experience marked the beginning of my unarticulated association of men's toilets with danger and with some kind of fearful, unspoken sexuality. In fact, tacitly she taught me two lessons that, as a child, I eventually lumped together. The first lesson was that male adults should not have sex with children. The second lesson was that males should not have sex with each other. Intellectually, I now separate the two lessons, accepting one and rejecting the other. At a deeper, wordless, emotional level, the two remain connected, like snails and oleander.

The connection I learned to make between public toilets and forbidden sexuality is unknowingly shared by many men. A fascinating question to ask students in class is "What do you do when you discover your stall is out of toilet paper?" Women report something like "Tap on the wall and ask the person next to you to provide some paper." Men say something like "Wait until the coast is clear and get some paper from the next stall."

Formal Education

By the time students reach college classrooms, most of them have deeply embedded understandings about sexuality—and other subjects of early learning—that are highly resistant to change. We teachers may lecture that researchers are not entirely sure why some people are erotically attracted to members of the opposite sex, some to their own sex, and a few to both sexes. We may remind students that these attractions sometimes change over time or as life situations change (Lips 1997). If, however, our students were taught at a very early age that being queer is shameful and that gay sex is disgusting, they will consider our suggestions intellectually, but they will generally retain their conflicting feelings of shame and disgust. (I recall a very "out" lesbian student who wrote that she was still made uncomfortable seeing men kiss.) Our students may simultaneously find our ideas intellectually plausible but emotionally unacceptable, as if we had given them a lecture on the nutritional value of eating snails.

Experiential and Rational Learning

The work of research psychologist Seymour Epstein (1994) provides another useful way of understanding what happens to students who appear on the surface to move in a positive direction intellectually but who retain their negative emotional reactions. Epstein theorizes that people simultaneously employ two different modalities, or systems of knowing: one associated with feeling (the experiential system) and one associated with intellectual ideas (the rational system). In ordinary speech, we often talk about "knowing with our heart" (i.e., emotionally) and "knowing with our head" (i.e., cognitively). According to Epstein, knowledge acquired by the experiential system is typically encoded in concrete images or spoken narratives, surrounded by strong feelings, broadly generalized, and experienced as self-evidently and categorically valid. Epstein writes that such knowledge "consist[s] primarily of generalizations derived from emotionally significant past experiences" that "automatically, rapidly, effortlessly, and efficiently processes information" (715). In contrast, knowledge acquired by the rational system is typically encoded in written words, logically connected, less emotional, more highly differentiated, and experienced actively as thoughts and ideas open to reconsideration. Epstein describes this as a "deliberative, effortful, abstract system that operates primarily in the medium of language . . . [which] is a very inefficient system for responding to everyday events" (715).

Most of what we learn in childhood is processed by the experiential system. Much of what we learn academically is processed by the rational system. Epstein observes that when information acquired by the rational system ("I think that homosexuality is acceptable") cannot be reconciled with information contained in the experiential system ("I feel that homosexuality is disgusting"), the rationally learned information is repressed in an effort to reduce conflict. The repressed anxiety may then be projected onto others (gays) who are seen as the cause of the distress.

We educators need to remind ourselves continually that students do not readily understand that their strong feelings about sexual orientation (as well as their ideas about race and gender) typically result from their early learning. They intuit and experience their disgust with gay sexuality as natural and normal. To make this point clearer, let me provide a nonthreatening example that I often use in class. As we watch a sunset, most of us "see" the sun "set" as it falls slowly below the horizon. If we take an astronomy class, we may learn that what we really see is the earth rotating away from the sun. Yet even astronomers who know that the earth rotates away from the sun may continue to "see" the sun "set" because that is what they learned experientially as children. What we have learned in error experientially in childhood persists as seeming more real than what we later learn rationally as adults.

The Heterosexual Bias

The heterosexual bias is the presumption, typically learned in early childhood, that any otherwise undefined person or relationship is presumptively heterosexual. Because the heterosexual bias is, in Epstein's terms, learned "experientially," it seems wholly natural. In uniformly describing families as "papa bear, mother bear, and the cubs," children's stories and fairy tales propagate the heterosexual bias. (Possibly the first children's book explicitly featuring a gay family was *Heather Has Two Mommies* [Newman 1989]). The heterosexual bias is similar to the male bias that presumes that an undefined individual is male. However, the male bias is often challenged, whereas the heterosexual bias is rarely challenged. As a writer, for example, I am reminded by my editor not to mindlessly employ the pronoun *he* when the referent could be either male or female, but I am not reminded to assume that this "he" might also be gay. Though society changes slowly, most people at least publicly contend that women and men should have equal rights (however loosely defined) and that girls should be able to pilot navy jets while men should be able to change diapers. Thoughtful writing, in its sensitivity to gender, reflects societal concern for heterosexual gender equality. But fewer people contend that gays should have equal rights and that they should be able to pilot navy jets and change diapers (Whitely and Kite 1995). This lack of sensitivity to sexual orientation reflects society's more general lack of concern for equality of sexual orientation.

The heterosexual bias takes many forms. A few years ago, for example, the president of the university where I teach, an intelligent and kindly man, asked me why gays needed to advertise their homosexuality. He asked why they could not just keep their sexual orientation private. I asked him whether or not he was advertising his heterosexuality by keeping a picture of himself and his wife on his desk, as well as permitting the new administration building to bear his and his wife's names. His response was one of puzzlement. In another example, a recent issue of *The New Yorker* (8 June 1997) critically reviewed a new biography of Cary Grant that highlights his zest for beautiful women but ignores entirely the fact that Grant was essentially homosexual. The heterosexual bias assumes that anyone as debonair as Cary Grant—or, to take another example, as rugged as Dallas Cowboys football player David Kopay (1977)—must be straight. The heterosexual bias supports the homosexual taboo when the bias permits people to studiously ignore gay lives and gay culture. Just as the heterosexual bias shielded the university president from seeing that the pictures on his desk made a statement about his own sexual orientation, and just as it kept the author of the Cary Grant biography from looking candidly at Grant's homosexual orientation, the bias helps keep the homosexual taboo untouched and intact. The heterosexual bias is maintained by group perception and thinking, which I will examine next.

Group Perception and Thinking

Teachers' efforts to enlighten student thinking about homosexuality are further hampered by group perception and group thinking. The perceptions and beliefs of students about sexuality, for example, are powerfully informed daily by the perceptions and beliefs of their peers and mentors. The power of the group to influence what an individual perceives was first tested scientifically by Solomon Asch in the early 1950s (Asch 1955). Asch placed a naive subject among a group of confederates and asked the naive subject to indicate which was the longest of three lines shown to him or her on a piece of paper. The test appeared very simple, because one of the three lines was clearly the longest. Yet the confederates consistently identified a short line as the longest. Under these circumstances, more than one-third of the naive subjects also chose the shorter line as the longest.

Asch's findings that such a large percentage of the subjects would immediately forgo their own perceptions were a shock to social psychologists, including Asch himself. It appeared that the fear of looking (being) different was enough to create conformity about simple perceptions. Studies by Stanley Schachter (1951) and others concluded that people do have a legitimate fear of looking different, because those who hold deviant views face being ostracized. In Schachter's study, a confederate participated in a group that was deciding the appropriate handling of a disciplinary matter. If the confederate agreed with the group consensus on what should be done, the group viewed him positively and included him in discussion. When the confederate took a contrary view, he was soon ignored and ostracized. Schachter concluded that groups tend to ostracize dissenters.

An understanding of the power of group thinking is vital to teachers in understanding the gay experience and student reaction to gay sexual orientation. Most straight students are continuously informed by significant segments of the society in which they live—their family, peers, school, and religion, as well as the media—that gay sexual orientation is morally wrong. If they think otherwise, they may fear that they face the threat of exclusion.

The Effect of Group Thinking on Gay Students

All children want and need to be accepted by their parents and by those who assume parental roles in children's lives. Children are accepted when they do that which is expected of them, such as telling the truth and being straight. Gay children learn at an early age to hide from their own instincts that tell them they are attracted to members of their own sex (Blumenfeld and Raymond 1993). They are ostracized for showing their feelings and rewarded for concealing them. As a result, gay people may feel unsure about something that ought to be quite obvious—their sexual orientation. In his poignantly moving account of growing up gay, Paul Monette (1992) recounts how, as a young man in college, he engaged in a series of heated, heterosexual love affairs in the forlorn hope that he could convince himself (and others) that he was straight. Though Monette "knew" from childhood that he was gay (in the way a child "knows" his or her sexual orientation), he continued to heed the voices of others who told him that he was not.

David Kopay, in his book *The David Kopay Story* (1977), describes how his macho appearance as a Dallas Cowboys football player led his unsuspecting friends and teammates to assume he was straight. When Kopay came out, many of them would not accept him, because they could not imagine that a gay man could play such a brutally aggressive game as professional football. Kopay's parents disowned him and moved to another state to avoid the shame they thought he had brought on them. Now, more than twenty years after Kopay came out, though his family has since reconciled, not a single other professional football player has ever followed Kopay's example (Young 1997).

My Beloved Jane

In contrast to the experience of Monette and Kopay, I remember a period in my childhood—perhaps I was about six years old—when I carried around a poster for the movie "The Outlaw" wherever I went. The poster featured a partially clad, very busty Jane Russell. I loved that poster. Although I seemed to have sensed that the poster made my mother uncomfortable, I also recall that she and my father were somewhat amused by my precocious heterosexuality. One can only imagine their reaction if my poster had featured a scantily dressed Rock Hudson.

Family Niches

Frank Sulloway, in his book *Born to Rebel* (1996), adds a final piece to our understanding of what it means to grow up gay. Sulloway utilizes Darwin's theory of natural selection to explain how an infant's instinctive need to survive leads him or her to use an adaptive strategy in fitting into available family niches. These niches tend to have certain consistent characteristics based on such factors as birth order, gender, socioeconomic class, and so forth. Sometimes these niches fit us well: a naturally assertive, outgoing child may be born into a family where the best available niche calls for an assertive and outgoing child.

What I find especially poignant in Sulloway's account is that the compulsion to adapt in order to survive requires many children to distort their true nature. Every family is designed with niches that welcome heterosexual children; very few are designed to welcome gay children. Virtually all gay children, as they grow up, feel pressured, even by well-meaning but uninformed or unsuspecting families, to be other than who they are sexually. Of course, children often do not meet parental expectations in other ways: a father hoping for a ballplayer may get a musician; a mother wanting a soul mate may get a politician instead. But the failure of children to meet these kinds of parental expectations is rarely as profound and as common as those regarding sexual orientation. Furthermore, gay children's beliefs that they have failed their parents in failing to meet their parent's expectation of heterosexuality only intensify the painful dilemma between living inauthentically in the closet or coming out and facing the risk of parental rejection.

Given the seemingly intractable resistance some students may have in thinking rationally about taboo subjects, such as homosexuality, what can teachers do to reach these students? The next section explores the theory of cognitive dissonance and the effect of what is called "counterattitudinal writing" in conjunction with experiential learning methods in fostering rational student thinking about homosexuality.

Part 2: Writing to Change Attitudes about Sexuality

Cognitive Dissonance

People learn from both external and internal sources. They learn from external sources when they attend lectures, read books, or talk to others. They learn from internal sources, so to speak, as they work mentally to assemble and organize this new information—a process called "adaptation," in Piagetian terms (see Inhelder and Piaget 1958). Often they discover that the newly acquired information conflicts with what was previously learned. Mentally adhering to conflicting or inconsistent thoughts or beliefs is called "cognitive dissonance." It leads to an unpleasant tension that can be relieved by changing one of the thoughts (Festinger 1957). For example, holding to the conviction that all people should have equal rights, such as the right to marry the person they love, while espousing the conflicting conviction that gays should not have such equal rights creates cognitive dissonance. Similarly, cognitive dissonance can exist between inconsistent thought and action. To avoid the dissonance, people tend to infer their own beliefs or thoughts from their own actions. If John frequently eats brown bread, he will infer that he likes brown bread. To infer otherwise would be to create dissonance. Accordingly, if Jane treats her gay colleague with respect, Jane will infer that she does respect her colleague.

To infer one's beliefs from one's behavior is part of self-perception theory (Bem 1972). For educators, the importance of the theories of cognitive dissonance and self-perception lies in their suggestion that, by intensifying the dissonance experienced by students in holding to inconsistent thoughts or inconsistent thoughts and actions, we can increase the chances of changing their attitudes. If we can change attitudes, we can broaden student thinking and writing. Writing plays an important role in intensifying dissonance. Although students can say conflicting things at different times without realizing they are doing so, they do not (ordinarily) write conflicting things, because the written word renders the difference more deliberate, more self-reflective, and more durable (Wade 1995). In short, when conflicting thoughts are expressed in writing, the dissonance is greater. Hence, a powerful way to persuade students to change their minds is to have them write the conflicting thoughts. One writing method that induces change through cognitive dissonance is called "counterattitudinal advocacy." This writing method, especially when combined with experiential teaching methods (as I will note shortly), is a powerful way to engage taboo thinking.

Counterattitudinal Advocacy

The notion behind counterattitudinal advocacy is simple: students asked to write an essay that counters their belief are more likely to change their minds, consistent with what they have written, than are students taught an opposing belief by conventional teaching methods (Miller et al. 1996). The method of counterattitudinal advocacy seems to have originated among psychology teachers as a means of countering intuitively held, naive beliefs among psychology students—such as their belief in extrasensory perception (ESP). Psychology students are perfectly free to believe in ESP at home in their spare time, so to speak, but in the classroom, they cannot accept ESP as a scientifically demonstrated phenomenon. To disabuse psychology students of their beliefs in ESP as a science, teachers ask them to write an essay on why the opposite of what they believe might be true.

The results of counterattitudinal writing are dramatic. A significantly greater percentage of students change their minds when they write a self-opposing view than when they merely hear lectures, read texts, or participate in discussions that present opposing views. Although different studies of conventional teaching methods vary, a summary of several studies suggests that if about 85 percent of psychology students at the beginning of a conventionally taught class have at least some belief in paranormal events, such as ESP, only about 50 percent will retain their beliefs at the end of the semester (Miller et al. 1996, 215). In one study, as an example, college students in a beginning psychology course were placed in one of three groups: the first group wrote a counterattitudinal essay; the second read and graded a counterattitudinal essay written by another student; and the third did neither, only being exposed to classroom lecture and/or textbook reading. All of the students in the study were asked to complete presemester and postsemester questionnaires that assessed their agreement with the scientifically accepted position on such paranormal phenomena as ESP. On a five-point scale, in which five points indicated agreement with the scientifically accepted position, the mean score of students who only read and graded the counterattitudinal essay moved from 1.8 to 3.3; the score of those who actually wrote counterattitudinal essays moved from 1.8 to 4.5; the score of the control group moved from 1.8 to 3.8. The differences in means between the group who did the counterattitudinal writing and the other two groups were all statistically significant at the .001 level (Miller et al. 1996).

The Ethics of Counterattitudinal Writing

Assigning students the task of writing against their intuitively held beliefs suggests an ethical dilemma: is counterattitudinal advocacy unethically coercive? One can attempt to circumvent the ethical issue by simply saying that all education is intrinsically coercive, because students are socialized by their schooling to tell their teacher what they think the teacher wants to hear: counterattitudinal writing is simply one more teaching device in an otherwise coercive system. Another way to hedge the ethical issue is to say that teachers present objective facts, about which students can make up their own minds. This approach—the argument that teachers merely impart facts or, at most, merely present different interpretations of facts in an evenhanded manner, so that students can decide for themselves—has been called the "cult of reason" (Brembeck and Howell 1967). The presumption of the cult of reason is that students engage in a thoughtful and rational analysis of what the teacher presents, so that the persuasive dynamics of the presentation are not at issue.

However, psychologists who study how students learn have demonstrated persuasively that the cult of reason is naive, in that however "objective" the content the teacher wishes to teach—one thinks of geometry as being objective—the teacher nonetheless plays a powerfully persuasive role in constructing and mediating how the material is to be taught. For example, geometry can be taught as evidence of the superiority of Western thinking, as proof that pure ideas exist, or as evidence that boys are better at math than are girls. Obviously, teaching about homosexuality is much less objective than geometry, and the ethical issues of persuasion are correspondingly that much greater.

The teacher's role in constructing and mediating how the material is taught is only half of the persuasion equation. The other half involves the student. Each student brings to the classroom a different set of life experiences. Teaching approaches that may be unpersuasive for one student may be highly persuasive to another. Teaching content that excites one student may leave another bored. Each student elaborates or adds to the content of what is taught, such that each student leaves the classroom with a different set of attitudes and beliefs. When the different ways in which teachers present even the most "objective" facts are combined with the highly idiosyncratic ways in which students process these facts, a totally unpredictable set of persuasive outcomes result.

Significant Choice: Four Standards of Ethical Teaching

"Significant choice" is an ethical approach to persuasive teaching that has attracted a number of writers (see Arnett 1991) and that I find helpful in designing my own teaching. Although these writers differ in detail and emphasis, they agree that significant choice entails at least four notions, or standards, that guide teachers in knowing how to teach in ways that are both persuasive and ethical: self-positioning, subject awareness, dissent encouragement, and appropriate outcome.

The first standard, self-positioning, involves respect—that is, that the teacher not only respects each student but openly states his or her personal biases and political agendas to all of the students. The teacher reveals these biases and agendas not so much to ensure that the students know where the teacher is coming from but so that students learn how to critically examine their sources of information. In teaching about gay issues, for example, I let students know of my involvement and support of the gay community.

The second standard is that the teacher keeps informed both of expertise in his or her subject area and also of the current political context in which the subject area is embedded. Even "objective" facts become value-laden as they are embedded in a larger political context. For example, marriage might look like an objective fact when viewed by a family law attorney concerned with a community property issue, but it might look like a highly value-laden and subjective issue when viewed from a gay perspective. The same "fact" of marriage would have conveyed wholly different values among preconquest North American Plains Indians, who recognized a sexual orientation among men *(berdache)* that sometimes led to a kind of homosexual marriage (Boswell 1981, 34). The teacher's setting also influences the objectivity of subject matter. What counts as an ethical issue of "persuasion" in my classroom in a Roman Catholic San Diego law school not only looks completely different from something we might imagine among the preconquest Plains Indians but would even look different were I teaching at a more "gay-friendly" law school, such as Cal Western Law School, located a scant four miles from my school.

The third standard to which the teacher should adhere in ethical teaching concerns means. It includes not only the teacher's acknowledgment of error and a classroom approach that avoids deception but also the teacher's encouragement of dissent. I sometimes find it difficult to meet the standard of encouraging dissent. I believe my teaching style openly encourages dissent, but I do not find it easy to support students' beliefs when they seem, to me, to be thoughtless adherence to religious dogma that stigmatizes homosexuality.

The fourth and final standard is targeting appropriate outcome, which means, somewhat paradoxically, that if a student gets the material "wrong" (e.g., if she or he still believes at the end of the semester that ESP is science or that all gay men have weak fathers and domineering mothers), she or he should get it wrong for the right reasons. If this student has, for example, heard the lecture, read the material, participated in the class discussions, completed his or her class project, and so forth, all in good faith, and still has it "wrong," the outcome is appropriate. Our ethical role as teachers is to educate (the English word comes from the Latin meaning "to lead forth"), not to coerce.

Part 3: Classroom Exercises to Broaden Attitudes about Gay Sexuality

In the first part of this chapter, I explained why I believe students experience difficulty in changing their views about homosexuality. In the second part, I offered a theoretical basis, along with an ethical analysis, for designing classroom exercises around counterattitudinal writing. In this part, I will illustrate how this writing approach, in conjunction with experiential exercises, can foster more open student thinking about homosexuality. The exercises were designed by my colleague Dr. Sharon Grodner and myself. We use experiential teaching methods, such as role plays, as the basis for writing, because of their clearly demonstrated advantages in modifying student attitudes (Zimbardo 1965). The exercises were designed primarily for an interviewing and counseling course in law school. Where appropriate, I will suggest how these exercises might be modified for courses outside of law school.

The Left-Handed Exercise

Our "left-handed exercise" applies both cognitive dissonance and self-perception theory. We introduce this exercise to the class by saying that we were going to talk about gay issues but thought that might be too controversial, so we decided instead to talk about being left-handed. We then ask if there are any left-handed people in class. (To avoid a dead-in-the-water exercise, check beforehand to make sure you have several left-handed students in your class.) We then ask a series of seemly innocuous, yet provocative, questions: How long have you been left-handed? Do your friends know? Is it genetic or learned? If genetic, should left-handers be permitted to marry? If learned, don't you set a bad example? Should school children be exposed to left-handed teachers? Should schools be mandated to provide left-handed scissors? Do you do everything left-handed? Don't you shake hands right-handed? Aren't there special stores for the left-handed? Have you shopped there? Don't special stores flaunt left-handedness? What do you think of the recent controversial study that left-handed people do not live as long as right-handed people? Doesn't that say something about your lifestyle? And why are there so many left-handed baseball pitchers? If you could be "cured" of your left-handedness by a therapist, would you undergo treatment?

Students begin to catch on that these questions, frequently asked of gays, sound foolish when asked of left-handers. They may argue that, unlike being gay, being left-handed has no social relevance. However, other students may counter that they had a left-handed parent or grandparent who was forced to change hands, often at a considerable cost. (My mother's teacher in grammar school required her to change hands and write with her right hand. She often said she thought that the change made her anxious in school and that handwriting was always stressful for her as a result.) Other students may know of some past societies in which left-handed infants were killed and of some present-day cultures in which eating in public is done only with the right hand. Some students may know that the words meaning "left" in French and Latin are *gauche* and *sinister*, respectively. Through this exercise, the analogy between the incidence and social consequences of sexual orientation and handedness begins to look meaningful to students.

Quick Writes and Anonymous Reads

At this point, we might invite students to do a "quick write." We invite them to write for three minutes on a topic we suggest. A good, all-purpose approach following any discussion is to ask students, "What would you have liked to say today that you did not?" At the end of three minutes, we ask the students to read silently what they have written and to decide if they are willing to have us read it aloud. If they are willing, we have them write "Read" at the top; if not, we have them write "Do not read." We collect the writings and read to the class those marked "Read." After we have completed the reading, we tear up all of the writings in class and dispose of them. When students see that we openly protect their anonymity, they are more likely to write candidly the next time.

Our quick-write feedback from students who have participated in the left-handed exercise suggests that this simple exercise can have a significant effect in changing student attitudes toward homosexuality.

Many students have never realized that left-handers form a relatively invisible minority (roughly the same percentage as gay people) and that they, too, feel discrimination and sometimes misunderstanding. The students see, on the one hand, that being left-handed would seem to be totally innocuous and, on the other hand, that it can and has had significant social consequences. Concerning both left-handedness and homosexuality, the dominant (right-handed and heterosexual) majorities make difference an issue.

Why the Left-Handed Exercise Works

The left-handed exercise may work because its message reaches students in three different ways. First, the exercise uses left-handedness as a kind of palatable surrogate for homosexuality. A student who may not be able to confront a classroom discussion on homosexuality (because of his or her strong, negative, taboo-related feelings) can deal with the apparent innocuousness of left-handedness. The exercise allows the student to empathize in easy stages with what it must be like to be left-handed, then invites him or her to explore an empathic connection with homosexuality. Second, the exercise avoids mind-numbing, intellectual debates about the nature of homosexuality, such as "nature" versus "nurture" arguments (Hamer and Copeland 1998). Arguments about whether homosexuality is genetic (nature) or learned (nurture), while certainly important in some contexts, serve as intellectual distractions that move students away from their feelings. Students can debate the nature of homosexuality until doomsday without ever exploring their feelings, let alone changing them.

Third, we create an open classroom environment that covertly counters the heterosexual bias by first overtly countering the "right-handed bias." Discussing left-handedness is nonthreatening. The questions we ask seem, at first, to be trivial. Yet most students soon understand that the questions are not trivial, because the bias against left-handedness is historically as prevalent and, in some ways, as damaging as the heterosexual bias. Finally, the exercise employs a counterattitudinal quick write. The writing is counterattitudinal because the left-handed exercise creates a mind-set in which a homophobic quick write would be cognitively dissonant. To write in a homophobic manner, the student would have to either distinguish left-handedness metaphorically from homosexuality or agree with the repression of left-handedness. In reading perhaps 150 (anonymous) quick writes following the left-handed exercise, I do not recall a single instance of overtly homophobic writing. This exercise attenuates the ethical issue implicit in counterattitudinal writing, because the writing is voluntary and anonymous.

Journals

I often assign weekly journal writing in my courses (see Hughes et al. 1997). I typically comment on the journals in the margin and return them to class the following week. Although students may write about anything they choose in their journals, I also provide weekly topics. Following the left-handed exercise, I have assigned as a possible topic "A Gay Friend." On the average, about half of the class will choose to write on this topic. These journals are among the most poignant and thoughtful I receive. One writer spoke of her "sarcastic and funny and successful and conservative and tasteful and smart and talented and gay" uncle. Another wrote about meeting her first gay couple, her boyfriend's brother and his partner, whom, she discovered, "are just like the many other married couples we know." She explained, "They bicker about dumb stuff, finish each other's sentences and steal a quick kiss during a brief, semiprivate moment." A third writer remembered how, as a child, a male couple took in her family in time of need. She writes: "I was too young to remember all of the circumstances. . . . To me, it did not matter. All that mattered is that those two men took wonderful care of me and my mother." I am presently collecting these journal stories (with the permission of the student writers) and hope to compose a reader from them. Journals may have the power to change student thinking, because they fit Epstein's model of experiential learning in that they involve concrete thinking and imagery embedded in a narrative context. The exercise employs an indirect, counterattitudinal approach, in that the assignment involves a friend. Writing about a friend invites a kindly, accepting approach and avoids negative stereotyping. A student writer who believes that all gay men are effeminate encounters cognitive dissonance in writing about a gay friend who is not. Writing about a friend attenuates the writers' possible taboo feelings about homoerotic thoughts. Friendships are assumed not to be sexual. The ethical issues implicit in counterattitudinal writing are again reduced because the choice of subject matter is voluntary.

The Reimagining Exercise

In our "reimagining exercise," we ask students to recall an event in their life that was memorable for some reason. The event might have been a family gathering, a school social occasion, an athletic event, or a vacation. We guide them through the imagery by asking them to recall the sights, sounds, and smells of the event. They then take several minutes to write down some key words or phrases that characterize the event. We then ask them to imagine the event a second time, only this time to assume that they had been gay. How might the event have changed? Finally, we ask them to describe the changed situation in a quick write. Again, we read these aloud anonymously with the writer's permission.

This exercise works well, I believe, because it is self-referential. The students start with their own lives and then, through their own imagination, we invite them to construct and write about a different life. The exercise feels safe to students (especially the men) because they retain control over the content. In hearing the stories their peers then tell in class, students experience the power of imaginal empathy in permitting them to experience life as others experience life. Both the left-handed exercise and the reimagining exercise are "safe" for gay students because the exercises protect their privacy to come out or not.

Once again, the exercise is counterattitudinal, because the students must write about themselves and are therefore motivated to conclude the story in a way that effectively integrates their newly attained, if imaginary, gay status. For example, one student's recollection was a Boy Scout ceremony, celebrating his attainment to Eagle Scout. In his imaginary acceptance speech, he triumphantly (if naively) comes out.

This exercise should work with students of high school age or older. The exercise also works using different themes. For example, instead of asking students to imagine they were gay, the teacher could ask them to imagine they were physically disabled, of the opposite gender, or of a different race.

Gay Role Play

We have found role plays to be effective in expanding student thinking. Even though role plays create only a brief experience under simulated conditions, the moment itself and the feelings generated are real. In one such exercise, we pair students arbitrarily as interviewers and interviewees and give them interview fact sheets. Each interviewer is told only that they are going to see a client with a problem. The interviewees are told that they have experienced the following scenario and are asked to share it with the interviewer.

> You were about to enter a bookstore several weeks ago when a young man came up to you and said belligerently, "I suppose you think you own this neighborhood!" You responded, "I don't know what you are talking about." At that point the young man suddenly gave you a push on the shoulder and you fell. The young man then jumped on a motorcycle, said something to the effect of "There are too many queers around here," and sped away. The young man seemed somehow familiar to you, and you now remember that he attends your school.

What interests us in the ensuing interview is whether the interviewer asks the interviewee about his or her sexual orientation. The "facts" provided in the interview instructions make it clear to most beginning law students that the interviewee has described an assault and battery. The assailant's motives in attacking a person he apparently perceived as gay may be very important in establishing either that the assault took place or, possibly, that the assault is also a "hate crime." If the assailant had used a racial or religious epithet, the interviewers would surely want to know, as a matter of course, whether the interviewee was a member of that race or religion. Yet some student interviewers will steadfastly ignore the issue of sexual orientation and will later argue that it is factually irrelevant. The exercise explores and reveals the student interviewers' discomfort with the taboo subject matter of homosexuality, such that he or she cannot inquire about it.

As with the other exercises, we follow this exercise with an anonymous quick write, in which we ask the participants to comment on the exercise. Generally, the interviewees report their surprise that they were not asked about their sexual orientation. Some of the interviewers, given anonymity and time to reflect, report that their anxiety kept them from asking the obvious questions. This exercise typically leads to a discussion about how to ask other questions that students may find discomforting, such as those about an interviewee's substance abuse, medications, or disabilities.

The exercise employs cognitive dissonance, because generally the interviewers ignore the client's sexual orientation as irrelevant while simultaneously asserting that they (typically "he") completed a legally competent interview. Writing intensifies the dissonance. The exercise utilizes a counterattitudinal approach, because it is virtually impossible for a student to write a cogent defense of avoiding the question of sexual orientation. Eventually, a student only looks foolish in defending his or her avoidance. Once again, the ethical issues attendant to counterattitudinal writing are minimized, because the writing is voluntary and anonymous.

Although we use this exercise in a law school setting, the legal aspects are not a necessary element. The interviewee might be seeking medical help, police help, or reporting to a community agency of some kind, including a school administrator's office. In each case, the relevance of the interviewee's sexual orientation will change, but the underlying anxiety about asking remains constant.

Conclusion

Students form their ideas about certain basics in life, such as their gender roles, sexual expression, race, and diet, in early childhood. Typically, these ideas are formed experientially, before much language is acquired. Ideas learned experientially in childhood are typically encoded in concrete images or narratives. These ideas are cloaked, so to speak, in a protective affect and are thereby experienced as "common sense," something beyond debate. When the surrounding affect is very strong, the protected idea may take on the appearance of a taboo. A taboo idea is not only resistant to change but cannot even be comfortably considered. Many students, especially male students, are homophobic to the extent that homosexuality has been emotionally walled off as a taboo topic. The taboo ideas of students, such as phobic ideas about homosexuality, can sometimes be accessed indirectly through nonthreatening exercises.

In doing these exercises, some students may find that the homophobic biases they have learned experientially early in life may be inconsistent with the notions of equality and fair play they have learned rationally. Holding to such inconsistent ideas creates a mental tension known as cognitive dissonance. The dissonance can be amplified, and the tension thereby increased, through writing. Counterattitudinal writing, in which a student writes an essay that counters his or her experientially held beliefs, maximizes the dissonance and has demonstrated success as a means of changing student thinking. Counterattitudinal writing may be especially powerful when it takes a narrative form that reflects an experiential mode of thinking. "Significant choice" doctrine provides guidelines for employing counterattitudinal writing ethically. The power of counterattitudinal writing to effect change may be amplified when combined with experiential teaching methods, in which students write about experience that has been generated in class through role play and other forms of simulation. Our goal with all of these teaching methods is to create a more just world.

Works Cited

Arnett, Ronald C. 1991. The status of communication ethics scholarship in speech communication journals from 1915 to 1985. In *Conversations on communication ethics,* ed. K. Greenberg, 55–72. Norwood, NJ: Ablex.

Asch, Solomon. 1955. Options and social pressure. *Scientific American* 11:32.

Bem, Daryl J. 1972. Self-perception theory. In *Advances in experimental social psychology,* ed. L. Berkowitz, 6: 127–32. New York: Academic.

Bem, Sandra Lipsitz. 1993. *The lenses of gender.* New Haven: Yale University Press.

Blumenfeld, Warren J., and Diane Raymond. 1993. *Looking at gay and lesbian life.* Boston: Beacon.

Boswell, John. 1981. *Christianity, social tolerance, and homosexuality.* Chicago: University of Chicago Press.

Brembeck, Warren L., and W. S. Howell. 1967. The ethics of persuasion. In *Ethics and persuasion,* ed. R. Johannesen, 3–27. New York: Random House.

Davis, Penelope J., and Gary E. Schwartz. 1987. Repression and the inaccessibility of affective memories. *Journal of Personality and Social Psychology* 52:155–62.

Epstein, Seymour. 1994. Integration of the cognitive and the psychodynamic unconscious. *American Psychologist* 49, no. 8:709–24.

Festinger, Leon. 1957. *A theory of cognitive dissonance.* New York: Harper and Row.

Hamer, Dean, and Peter Copeland. 1998. *Living with our genes.* New York: Doubleday.

Hudson, Liam, and Bernadine Jacot. 1991. *The way men think: Intellect, intimacy, and erotic imagination.* New Haven: Yale University Press.

Hughes, Herman Woodrow, Mary Kooy, and Lannie Nanevsky. 1997. Dialogic reflection and journaling. *Clearing House* 70, no. 4 (March–April): 187–91.

Inhelder, Barbel, and Jean Piaget. 1958. *The growth of logical thinking from childhood to adolescence.* New York: Basic.

Kopay, David. 1977. *The David Kopay story.* New York: Arbor House.

Laing, R. D. 1971. *The politics of the family.* New York: Vintage.

Lips, Hillary. 1997. *Sex and gender.* Mountain View, CA: Mayfield.

Miller, Richard L., William J. Wozniak, Marci R. Rust, Beverly R. Miller, and Jennifer Slezak. 1996. Counterattitudinal advocacy as a means of enhancing instructional effectiveness: How to teach students what they do not want to know. *Teaching of Psychology* 23, no. 4:215–19.

Monette, Paul. 1992. *Becoming a man: Half a life story.* New York: Harcourt Brace Jovanovich.

Money, John. 1980. *Love and love sickness: The science of sex, gender difference, and pair bonding.* Baltimore: Johns Hopkins University Press.

Newman, Leslea. 1989. *Heather has two mommies.* New York: Alyson.

Schachter, Stanley. 1951. Deviation, rejection, and communication. *Journal of Abnormal Psychology* 46:190–207.

Sulloway, Frank J. 1996. *Born to rebel: Birth order, family dynamics, and creative lives.* New York: Pantheon.

Trevarthen, Colwyn. 1995. Contracts of mutual understandings: Negotiating meanings and moral sentiments with infants. *Journal of Contemporary Legal Issues* 6:373–406.

Wade, Carole. 1995. Using writing to develop and assess critical thinking. *Teaching of Psychology* 22, no. 1:24–8.

Whitely, Bernard E., Jr., and Mary E. Kite. 1995. Sex differences in attitudes toward homosexuality: A comment on Oliver and Hyde. *Psychological Bulletin* 117, no. 1 (January): 146–54.

Young, Perry Dean. 1997. Twenty years later, Bryant crusade still fueling gay-rights debate. *Chapel Hill Herald,* 15 February, see B, p. 3.

Zimbardo, Philip G. 1965. The effect of effort and improvisation in self-persuasion produced by role-playing. *Journal of Experimental Social Psychology* 1, no. 2:103–20.

Zinsser, William. 1988. *Writing to learn.* New York: Harper and Row.

Chapter Nine

Afterword: Reading and Writing Diversity

Min-Zhan Lu
Drake University
Des Moines, IA

For me, this volume is instructive for several reasons. It confirms my belief in the centrality of writing in our daily efforts to understand and construct the meaning of "multiculturalism" or "cultural diversity" inside and outside college classrooms. It illuminates the need for a dialogue among those of us who teach across the disciplines, as we develop pedagogies that attend not only to the question of what we should assign our students to read and write about but also to the question of how we should ask them to read and write. More specifically, the volume offers an opportunity for us to hear from members in the communities of education, sociology, English composition, anthropology, ethnic studies, law, and so forth as they explore ways of reading and writing that treat cultures as interactive forces, rather than as discrete entities, and as dynamic processes actively shaped by real historical agents in response to specific material conditions. This dialogue is all the more instructive because of the contributors' attention to the "nuts and bolts" of teaching: the challenging (but often underappreciated) work teachers put into designing assignments, developing grading policies, or interacting with individual students both in and outside the classroom, as well as the philosophies of language and culture underlying diverse pedagogies. This volume enacts a model for exploring the complex relationship between theory and practice as we participate in the continuing debates over issues of diversity and multiculturalism.

I want to map out here two of the many conversations I hear emerging from these essays. One conversation explores how we read and write about the texts and contexts that traditionally have been overlooked by the academy—the need to acknowledge the agency of the oppressed and to highlight the link among the individual, the collective, culture, and history. In "Recognizing Diversity within a Common Historical Narrative: Culture, History, and the Study of Social Life," John Wills and Hugh Mehan use the material from their studies of practices in fourth-grade and eighth-grade history classrooms to argue that to make our curriculum more diverse or multicultural, we need not only to assign students history books by and about members of "minority" cultures but also to examine how we present "history" and "culture" through our teaching methods. For instance, their studies found that an eighth-grade course in U.S. history produced student essays, class discussions, and exercises that continued to treat whites and Native Americans as distinctive "cultures" and "peoples"—artifacts existing outside specific historical time—rather than as active historical agents engaged in struggles over civil rights. Wills and Mehan therefore urge us to examine how we teach our students to read historical events and history books, as well as what kind of stories we tell about these books and events. They urge that we promote ways of reading and writing that treat history as something made in interaction among diverse cultural groups struggling for civil rights against the facts of gender, ethnic, and racial discrimination at a given historical time. Instead of reducing "cultures" and "peoples" to distinctive food, clothing, music, and artifacts or to lists of major figures, they argue that we need to focus our attention on individual and collective agency. Wills and Mehan conclude that "teachers need to recognize that, along with their students, they are constructing a narrative of events about the struggle for rights that constitutes U.S. history."

Tom Fox's essay, "From Freedom to Manners: African American Literacy in the Nineteenth Century," and Gail Pérez's essay, "The View from Here: Toward a Critical Pedagogy in the Multiethnic Classroom," indicate that both authors perceive themselves as active makers of history. Each offers a concrete example of how to construct alternative stories about texts and events that have been overlooked by previous institutional practices but that are nevertheless central to our understanding of the local and national history of one's discipline—literacy studies and ethnic studies. Both illustrate the impact such alternative history making can have not only on our understanding of the past but also on action taken in the present by both teachers and scholars.

Fox reads historical documents—protest literature by pre–Civil War slaves, political pamphlets, slave narratives, court petitions of emancipation, written accounts of slave rebellions, and textbooks available to freedmen in the years following the Civil War—to foreground the individual and collective agency of African American slaves in their struggle for rights to literacy and freedom. His approach exemplifies the kind of reading and writing that I believe Wills and Mehan would like to see produced in the history classrooms they study. For instance, Fox begins with a rhetorical analysis of David Walker's "Appeal in Four Articles" ([1848] 1969), including Walker's decision to address his article to "Colored Citizens" and to make an unrelenting assertion of African American humanity and power. Instead of treating such textual moves as self-contained features distinctive to a genre of writing, Fox reads them in connection to the specific contexts of slavery, in terms of Walker's attempt to place the issues of freedom and liberty beyond the control of white readers and into the hands of an assumed literate slave audience. Fox further links these textual forms to the commotion—anxiety and fear—that Walker's writing caused among white slaveholders, to call attention to the real, historical impact such textual moves had on the slaves' struggle against slavery. Fox likewise reads nineteenth-century textbooks, such as *The Freedmen's Book* by Child ([1865] 1968), to examine the extent to which their content and rhetoric acknowledge the cruelty of slave owners, the resistance of slaves, and the interests of ex-slaves in achieving racial, economic, and political equality through education. He thus presents such historical documents as having material impact both on the efforts of a federal agency—the Freedmen's Bureau—to use formal schooling to make ex-slaves more submissive, industrious, and accepting of the conditions of oppression during Reconstruction and on the resistance of the freedmen and their struggle to use education as a means for broader political and economic emancipation. Instead of treating freedmen as passive victims of the Freedmen's Bureau or of textbooks advising them to trade in political action for planter boxes in front of their homes, Fox urges us to look to historical texts and events for evidence that indicates the resistance of freedmen—for proof of their efforts to set up black-initiated, black-run schools to further their capacity to restructure their lives and establish their freedom. Fox's reading of the literacy history of African Americans in the nineteenth century is in keeping with an interest, in the field of composition studies, to develop pedagogies that foreground the politics of style and the political agency of the receiver, as well as the producer, of writing and learning. His essay illustrates the pedagogies' potential in helping future teachers across the disciplines to develop the kind of multicultural classrooms projected by Wills and Mehan.

Fox also poses a model for writing history that contests, rather than confines itself to, established institutional boundaries, including the tendency to exclude "nonacademic writing"—such as the literacy practices of African Americans during the nineteenth century—in formal histories of writing and rhetoric. Fox's concern to write the "undiscoursed" history of composition intersects with Pérez's effort to tell a story "generally obscured" in historical accounts of the women's studies program and Chicano studies department at San Diego State University: both programs drew support from local, community activism. Noting that ethnic studies, literacy programs, and community service are increasingly becoming bureaucracies and academic industries (often funded by foundations), Pérez talks to local activists to recall a history in the development of these programs at San Diego State University, when ethnic content, radical pedagogy, and grassroots movements were "woven into an organic whole." Besides setting up a model for producing alternative histories, both Fox and Pérez consider the impact their history making can have on the current and future formation of their discipline. Fox urges us to use the history of African Americans' heroic commitment to literacy during and after slavery, first, to confront formal literacy education's failure to generate social or political power for African Americans and, then, to reform the structure of formal education. By contesting the stereotypical view that African Americans "live in an 'oral culture,'" or in a culture that does not support education, this new history should also motivate us to reform our attitudes toward African American students and their home cultures, both inside and outside the classroom. Pérez likewise links her research on the local history of Chicano studies and women's studies programs with her current work in ethnic studies programs and her position toward the false dichotomy between scholarship and activism in current debates within these fields. She draws impetus for her efforts to involve students and local activists in developing a pedagogy that treats "service learning" as "service for change"—a transformative pedagogy that creates awareness and changes social relations through activism. In such a pedagogy, ethnic texts are taught in order to unpack the web of contradictions their presence in our schools reveals and, thus, to create reasons for transforming educational settings and practices.

In challenging stereotypes of African American culture and African American people as "oral," or as uninterested in education, Fox's writing also reminds us, as Wills and Mehan put it, to view racial, ethnic, or gender identities as fluid processes that emerge in interaction and in struggle for civil rights, rather than as sets of fixed characteristics. Instead of beginning with people's ethnic or racial identity (as practiced in the history classrooms studied by Wills and Mehan), we need to begin with society, which, of necessity, will turn our attention to how racial and ethnic identities are constituted in social life. We see the same assumptions operating in Franklin Ng's "Exploring Diversity in the Writings of Asian American Students," even though one of Ng's explicit goals is to encourage his students to write about "topics of personal interest." Ng encourages his students to write about such topics and to "value their own voices, their own memories, and their own narratives," not only because he perceives these pedagogical moves as the best way of helping them overcome their anxiety about writing, but also because he perceives these moves as the best way of guiding students to conduct the kind of "reflexive thinking" he wants to engage them in, thinking that treats the "personal" as shaped by and shaping the collective—social and historical—and that questions the students' assumptions along with the assumptions of their communities and the larger society. From the ways in which Ng encourages his students to draw on library research, oral interviews, personal experience, and reflections to produce "thick description" from topics of their interest, I note a pedagogy that, like the radical pedagogy Pérez poses, allows students to see their interests (or identities) as a part of history, with a past and a potential future as well as a present, and that encourages students to use writing to understand and change their relationships to history and, hence, their own identities.

For instance, when discussing second-generation students' yearning for the home-cooked dishes that their parents made and their interest in collecting recipes, Ng directs the students' attention to a series of food-related literacy and social actions taken by Asian immigrants in their struggle in U.S. society and history. In the process, Ng encourages his students to read these texts and events to foreground the inventive and resourceful efforts of both the individual and the collective: community groups put out cookbooks to transmit to later generations the customs, folk wisdom, or remedies of home cultures. As examples of transmission of culture, Ng cites Cambodian refugees' use of the spelling *donut* instead of *doughnut* to save money for shop signs, as well as shopowners' offering of seemingly incompatible food items—donuts, hamburgers, and Chinese food—to maximize their business potential for a diverse clientele. This kind of teaching implicitly guides students to approach ethnic trends—their own yearning for specific types of cooking; the food preferences or preparations of ethnic groups; and "ethnic occupational specialization," such as Cambodian donut shops throughout California—as constructed and reconstructed in response to very specific social and historical conditions, including conflicts between past and present and between "American" and "South Asian" values, beliefs, and perspectives. I identify the guidance as implicit because this approach is built in the way Ng talks about the examples he uses when helping students to develop their topic, rather than being explicitly stated in his course material. Furthermore, as Ng points out, many of his students "do not necessarily see ethnicity as being situational or nonlinear, or as an identity that may be constructed and reconstructed through time." In fact, their discourses and narratives reveal a vast array of perspectives, including ethnocentrism, immigrant nationalism, acceptance of racial hierarchies, class bias, indifference to discrimination, and a preference for assimilation as opposed to multiculturalism. Ng opts for "the Tao of openness" toward the opinions and ideas his students produce in the process of "reflexive thinking." I believe he opts for this openness exactly because he perceives, as illustrated by his readings of signs on donut shops and of cookbooks put out by community groups, that "values, beliefs, and persons"—American or Asian American—are unstable and actively constituted through individual and collective efforts to question one's own assumptions and the assumptions of the community and larger society. Therefore, as Ng argues, it is more important for educators to provide "examples, illustrating the directions [students] could take and the questions they could raise" while helping them develop topics of "personal interest," than to serve as gatekeepers on where students start (the topic) and what they find (the ideas they come up with) in the process.

This position echoes the concern of Steven Hartwell in "Out of the Closet: Writing to Learn," when he makes the fourth standard of ethical thinking the effort to target "appropriate outcome, which means, somewhat paradoxically, that if a student gets the material 'wrong' (e.g., if she or he still believes at the end of the semester that ESP is science or that gay men have weak fathers and domineering mothers), she or he should get it wrong for the right reasons." That is, the "wrong" outcome is appropriate if the student has followed the "right" directions and explored the questions posed by the teacher. The core of a curriculum lies in how we think, read, and write about the relations between the individual, collective, cultural, and historical.

Another, related conversation emerging from the essays in this volume centers on how to help students become more reflective about the frames of reference they use when exploring diversity. Fox and Pérez reread the history of their disciplines by reflecting on the assumptions dominating previous readings from similar professional locations. In short, to better understand the perspectives of another "culture" or "people," it is also better to understand the limitations and strengths of the frames of reference one habitually brings to people and cultures different than one's "own" and to locate these frames of reference on the social, historical map. One must learn to take responsibility for the locations and frames of reference one chooses in future actions. This seems to be the issue of concern in various discussions of assignment design throughout the volume. For instance, Mark L. Waldo and Amanda Espinosa-Aguilar, in "Linking Assignment Design to Paper Grading in Classes about Diversity," are concerned that since there are rarely clear-cut answers to issues of diversity, responsible grading would have to be accompanied by careful design of writing assignments and discussions of assignments. They urge teachers to design assignments that pose questions about which students can think critically; that provide "engaging context, locating [students] in some pertinent situation in which to write"; and that offer "an identifiable audience." Among the examples they use is an assignment from an introductory physics course, where a physics major living in Reno is asked to explain to his precollege brother living in New York why a three-minute soft-boiled egg would take longer to cook in a geographical location that is nearly a mile above sea level. If we examine this physics assignment, along with the "positioning pieces" offered by Terri Hasseler and John Bean in "Designing Writing Assignments for Exploring Diversity," we might say that the criteria for assignment writing posed by Waldo and Espinosa-Aguilar are "good" because they implicitly call students' attention to the ways in which "location" affects our understanding of diversity.

Hasseler and Bean cite Adrienne Rich (1984) to emphasize the political nature of "location" or "position": "a place on the map is also a place in history within which as a woman, a Jew, a lesbian, a feminist I am created and trying to create." They argue that positioning pieces can help students recognize the constructed nature of the frame of reference or the positional lens through which any given person sees the world. Positioning assignments differ from narrative autobiographical pieces in that they ask students to analyze multiple and conflicting elements of identity in a way that de-centers the self. These assignments immerse students in the tensions and complications of their own identities and invite them to accept responsibility for their position in the world. In identifying a context and audience for the student, the physics assignment likewise requires the student to take a position in a social as well as geographical map, in relation to competing discursive locations—academic versus nonacademic, physics versus nonscientific—and to differing geographical locations. It thus invites the student to view "knowledge" as constructed through interaction across diverse perspectives and in response to very specific and material—social as well as environmental—conditions. A student who has been taught physics through this type of assignment would be better prepared to do work in Ng's classroom and in classrooms that use "position pieces" similar to the ones offered in Hasseler and Bean. The reverse situation would also be true: a student who has completed work in Ng's classroom or position pieces like those offered by Hasseler and Bean would be better prepared for the physics assignment presented by Waldo and Espinosa-Aguilar. As Steve Hartwell illustrates by using his own teaching experiences, seemingly neutral topics, such as left-handedness, are useful segues into "controversial" topics, such as gay rights and homophobia. To engage students in exploring diversity in terms of racial, ethnic, class, gender, and sexual differences, we need more science classrooms that encourage students to view seemingly neutral, "scientific" perspectives in terms of social location and in relation to issues of diversity. As Hartwell reminds us, writing can play an important role in intensifying dissonance. Although students can say conflicting things at different times without realizing they are doing so, the written word renders the difference more deliberate, more self-reflective, and more durable. A powerful way to persuade students to change their minds is to have them write the conflicting thoughts. This seems to be the purpose of one assignment included among the position pieces by

Hasseler and Bean, an exercise that asks students to use three-columned writing to reflect on the lenses they and others use to view differences. Such a writing exercise might be used to help students who define themselves in terms that transcend ethnic, gender, sex, or class categories (as "intellectual," "energetic," or "bubbly") to confront the dissonance between how they perceive themselves and how they perceive others and to change their locations in relation to all systems of discrimination. This type of reading and writing would serve equally well those students who find themselves in classrooms informed by the philosophy of identity, language, culture, and history posed by Wills and Mehan, Pérez, and Fox.

In trying to capture two of the many conversations I hear across the essays included in this volume, I find myself barely touching on the wealth of insights each piece has to offer. This sense of inadequacy itself is, I believe, a comment on the quality of the individual contributions and of the volume's overall contribution to our thinking on issues of diversity and multiculturalism. Phyllis Kahaney and Judith Liu have done the profession a real service in putting this fine volume together.

WORKS CITED

Child, Lydia Maria. [1865] 1968. *The Freedmen's book.* Reprint, New York: Arno.

Rich, Adrienne. 1984. Notes toward a politics of location. In *Blood, bread, and poetry,* 210–31. New York: Norton.

Walker, David. [1848] 1969. *Appeal in four articles.* Reprint, New York: Arno.

Contributors

John C. Bean is a professor of English at Seattle University, where he has the official title of Consulting Professor for Academic and Professional Writing. He has been active in the Writing across the Curriculum movement since 1976 and is the author of *Engaging Ideas: The Professor's Guide to Writing, Critical Thinking, and Active Learning in the Classroom* (1996). He is also coauthor of two textbooks: *The Allyn and Bacon Guide to Writing,* second edition (2000); and *Writing Arguments,* fifth edition (2001).

Amanda Espinosa-Aguilar is an Assistant Professor of English and the Writing Center Director at Washington State University, Tri-Cities. She teaches classes in rhetorical theory, composition, autobiography, and ethnic American literature. She has presented papers at the national conferences of the Modern Languages Association, Conference on College Composition and Communication, National Council of Teachers of English, and National Writing Centers Association. Her research interests are varied but focus on tracing the use of anger as a rhetorical device in ethnic American autobiography and literature. Her publications include "Resources for Teaching Latino Literature," *Making Connections: A Journal for Teachers of Culturally Diverse Literatures* 4, no. 1 (Fall 1999): 4–6; "The Colonial Rhetoric of English Only," *Language Ideologies: Critical Perspectives on the Official English Movement,* 2d ed., ed. Roseann Duenas Gonzalez (NCTE: Urbana, 2000); "Outside the Inner Circle: My Experiences as a Minority in Academia," *The Write Connection* 5, no. 2 (April 1992): 4–5, and a variety of reviews, short stories, and poems.

Tom Fox is a professor of English at California State University, Chico. He regularly teaches first-year writing, as well as graduate and undergraduate courses in composition. He directs the Northern California Writing Project and helps coordinate university composition programs. He is the author of *The Social Uses of Writing* (1990) and *Defending Access* (1999), he is coeditor of *Writing With: New Directions in Collaborative Teaching, Learning, and Research* (1994), and he has written many articles on the intersections of composition and culture.

Steven Hartwell is a clinical professor of law at the University of San Diego. Previously, he served as a Peace Corps volunteer in Kenya and as regional director in Colombia. Later, he served as director and senior attorney for the Legal Aid Society of San Diego. He teaches courses in negotiating, trial practice, and interviewing and counseling, as well as cross-disciplinary courses in gender and family therapy. Among other publications, he has written about gay issues on "What a Difference a Gay Makes: An Empirical Study of the Impact of 'Out' Gay Law Instructors in Law School Curriculum and Policy," *National Journal of Sexual Orientation Law* 1, no. 2 (1995): 227–34; about law and family therapy in "Beyond Law and Ethics: An Interdisciplinary Course in Family Law and Family Therapy," with Patti Riley, George Sargent, and JoEllen Patterson, *Journal of Marital and Family Therapy* 23, no. 1 (1997): 461–76; about gender and negotiating in "Women Negotiating: Assertiveness and Relatedness," with Roger Pace, in *Constructing and Reconstructing Gender*, edited by Linda A. M. Perry, Lynn H. Turner, and Helen M. Sterk (1992); and about moral development in "Promoting Moral Development through Experiential Teaching," *Journal of Clinical Education* 505 (Spring 1995): 505–39. In 1991, he helped found Pride Law, which represents the interests of gay law students, and he has served as its faculty advisor since its inception.

Terri A. Hasseler is an assistant professor of English and coordinator of the women's studies program at Bryant College. Her research interests include postcolonial literature, particularly literature of the Indian diaspora and Victorian literature.

Phyllis Kahaney was an assistant professor of English and the director of the Writing Program at the University of San Diego and at the University of Hawaii, Hilo. She is coeditor of *Theoretical and Critical Perspectives on Teacher Change*, with Linda A. M. Perry and Joseph Janangelo (1993); and coauthor of "Journal Writing as Social Interaction: Writing to Learn in the Workplace," with Kathleen Heinrich, in the *Interdisciplinary Handbook of Adult Lifespan Learning* (1994). She is now a research specialist at the San Diego State University Foundation, where her research interests include the elderly and the chronically ill.

Judith Liu is a professor of sociology at the University of San Diego, where she teaches theory and gender courses. Her research interests include missionary education in China, multicultural education in the United States, and pedagogy. She has coauthored *The Ethnographic Eye: Interpretive Studies of Education in China* (2000) and has written articles on women and HIV/AIDS, comparative education, and critical pedagogy.

Min-Zhan Lu is an endowment professor of the humanities at Drake University, where she teaches courses in writing, autobiography, fiction, and critical theory. Her scholarship is concerned with the use of cultural dissonance in teaching and with the politics of representing difference.

Hugh Mehan is a professor of sociology and the director of the Center for Research on Educational Equity and Teaching Excellence (CREATE) at the University of California, San Diego, positions that link his commitments to research and practice. He has authored four books (*The Reality of Ethnomethod-*

ology [1975], *Learning Lessons* [1979], *Handicapping the Handicapped* [1986], and *Constructing School Success* [1996]) and has edited four books (*Language Use and School Performance* [1973], *The Right Help* [1986], *The Social Organization of Intellectual Behavior* [1980], and *The Discourse of the Nuclear Arms Race* [1988]). Recently elected to the National Academy of Education, he has received three teaching awards at the University of California, San Diego: the Academic Senate's Outstanding Teacher Award in 1997, the Thurgood Marshall College Outstanding Teaching Award in 1991, and the Eleanor Roosevelt College Outstanding Teaching Award in 1994.

Franklin Ng is a professor of anthropology at California State University, Fresno. His interests include Asian Pacific Americans, international history, and American–East Asian cultural relations. He is a coauthor of the Houghton Mifflin History and Social Studies series (1999) approved for the California schools. He is also the editor of *The Asian American Encyclopedia* (1995) and author of *The Taiwanese Americans* (1998).

Gail Pérez received her Ph.D. from Stanford University, where she was also a Wallace Stegner fellow in creative writing. She is presently an assistant professor at the University of San Diego, where she cofounded the ethnic studies minor. Her scholarly interests include critical pedagogy, creative writing, Chicana literature, and the literature of women of color. Believing that activism and scholarship go hand in hand, she is involved in many organizations along the U.S.-Mexican border that seek to bring social justice to an emerging, multiethnic California.

Mark L. Waldo is the director of the Writing Center and a professor of English at the University of Nevada, Reno. His most recent publications have appeared in *Writing Centers and Writing across the Curriculum Programs* (1999) and *Journal of Criminal Justice Education* 8, no. 1 (1997). He is currently at work on a book that combines many of his professional and personal interests: writing across the curriculum, writing centers, composition studies, writing assessment, nineteenth-century British literature, and air-mattressing white-water rivers.

John S. Wills is an assistant professor in the Graduate School of Education at the University of California, Riverside. His publications include "Who Needs Multicultural Education? White Students, U.S. History, and the Construction of a Usable Past," *Anthropology and Education Quarterly* 27, no. 3 (1996): 365–89; "Recognizing Diversity within a Common Historical Narrative: The Challenge to Teaching History and Social Studies," with Hugh Mehan, *Multicultural Education* 4, no. 1 (1996): 4–12; "Ethnographic Studies of Multicultural Education in Classrooms and Schools," with Hugh Mehan, Angela Lintz, and Dina Okamoto, in *Handbook of Research on Multicultural Education*, edited by James A. Banks and Cherry A. McGee Banks (1995); and "Popular Culture, Curriculum, and Historical Representation: The Situation of Native Americans in American History and the Perpetuation of Stereotypes," *Journal of Narrative and Life History* 4, no. 4 (1994): 277–94. His research interests are the politics of curriculum and school knowledge, the representation and narration of history in schools and classrooms, history/social studies education, and multicultural education. His areas of teaching include the sociocultural foundations of education, multicultural education, qualitative research methods, curriculum theory, and the sociology of education.

Index